The American Horse

The Horse in United States History

BROUGHT TO YOU BY

The books created by Equine Heritage Institute are designed to preserve the history and majesty of the horse. Our goal is to find, understand, and pass on the valuable data about equine use and its influence on humanity. The Equine Heritage Institute is a not for profit 503(c) and 100% of all proceeds from the sale of books, services, and products support Equine Heritage Institute's mission.

To make a donation to EHI, please visit www.ehi-donations.com

SPECIAL THANKS TO OUR TEAM

Mary Chris Foxworthy, Research Writer

Mary Chris' grandfather owned one of the last creameries in the United States that still used horse-drawn milk wagons. This sparked her life-long love affair with horses and passion for keeping horse history alive. After graduating from college with a degree in Food Science and Communications, Mary Chris bought her very first horse with her first paycheck. Since then, she has served on the board of various equine associations and held a judge's card in Carriage Driving. She is known for her work in the Gloria Austin Collection, and has published and presented numerous equine educational programs. She has written for several equine publications and won an award from American Horse Publications for one of her articles. Mary Chris is an active exhibitor in Carriage Driving and Dressage. Along with her husband, she enjoys spending time with their horses (two Morgans and a PRE), a bouncing Bearded Collie and two adult children and one grandchild.

Abby David, Graphic Designer

Abby David's family has roots in the Walking Horse tradition and she grew up hearing tales of Ole Tobe the mule's antics, holiday wagon decorations, and trick riding. In her teens she spent her summers boarding the neighbors horses and playing at barrel racing in the back paddock with Thunder. She landed a job as a Graphic Designer at The Arts Center of Cannon County in 2004 and has worked in the print and digital mass communications industry continuously. Since marrying into a family in the racehorse business, she has enjoyed exploring a whole new world of horses and wearing big fancy hats. She also enjoys dancing in all it's forms and teaches in her local community.

Gloria Austin's Collection of Books

www.GloriaAustin.com

ENJOY OUR OTHER BOOKS

- How a Horse Can Make You a Better Dancer
- The Brewster Story
- Carriage Lamps
- A Glossary of Harness Parts
- Equine Elegance
- The Fire Horse
- Horse Basics 101
- The Unsung Heros of World War One
- The Horse, History, and Human Culture
- Horse Symbolism
- Horses of the Americas
- A Drive Through Time: Carriages, Horses, and History
- The Medieval Horse
- Speak Your Horse's Language
- The Golden Carriage and the House of Hapsburg
- Women and Horses
- A Cookbook for Horse Lovers
- Dance! To Improve Riding and Driving
- Horses and Newport
- Coaches, Carriages, and Carts

Brought To You By The Equine Heritage Institute

The American Horse
By: Gloria Austin
President of the Equine Heritage Institute, Inc. (EHI)

First Publish Date August 2020
Copyright © 2020 by Equine Heritage Institute, Inc.
All rights reserved. No part of this publication may be reproduced, distributed, or transmitted in any form or by any means, including photocopying, recording, or other electronic or mechanical methods, without the prior written permission of the publisher, except in the case of brief quotations embodied in critical reviews and certain other noncommercial uses permitted by copyright law. For permission requests, write to the publisher, addressed "Attention: Permissions Coordinator," at the address below.

Gloria Austin Carriage Collection, LLC; Equine Heritage Institute, Inc.
3024 Marion County Road Weirsdale, FL 32195 Office: (352) 753-2826 Fax: (352) 753-6186

Ordering Information:
Quantity sales: Special discounts are available on quantity purchases by corporations, associations, and others. For details, contact the publisher at the address above.
Printed in the United States of America First Edition
ISBN: Print 978-1-951895-08-2, E-Book 978-1-951895-07-5

Table of Contents

Foreward 8
Introduction 12
Early Settlers and Explorers 13
   Hunting 14
   Farming 14
   Transportation and Communication 15
   Ranching 15
   Commerce 16
   Racing 17
   Conquests 18
Types of Horses in Early America 19
Colonial Times 21
The Horse and the Fight for Freedom 24
   The Use of the Horse in the
      American Revolution 24
   Famous Horses and Riders of the Revolution 27
The Horse and the Advancing Frontier 31
   The Wilderness Road 31
   Lewis and Clark 33
   The Impact of Agricultural Inventions 34
   Gold! 35
   Western Expansion Getting There 36
   Settling the West 39
   Transportation 40
   Communication 42
   Ranching 43
   Mining 45
   Farming 46
   Railroads 49
   Native Americans 50
   The Aura of the West 51
Civil War 52
   The Use of the Horse in the American
      Civil War 52
   Famous Horses and Riders of the Civil War 57
The Growth of Cities 60
   Horse Relics Still Found in Cities 61
   Urbanization - The Population
      Shift to the Cities 63
   So Many People with So Many Needs 65
World War I 74
On the Move Without Horses 78
Horse Breeds of America 79
   American Paint Horse 79
   American Quarter Horse 80
   American Saddlebred 82
   Appaloosa 83
   Banker Ponies 85
   Carolina March Tacky 86
   Chickasaw 87
   Choctaw and Cherokee 88
   Chincoteague Ponies 90
   Conestoga Horse 91
   Florida Cracker Horse 92
   Missouri Fox Trotter 93
   Morgan 94
   Mustang 98
   Narragansett Pacer 99
   Rocky Mountain Horse 101
   Standardbred 103
   Tennessee Walker 105
   Thoroughbred 106
The Horse in America Today 108
Sources 118

The Horse

"We have had 6,000 years of history with the domesticated horse and only 100 years with the automobile."

Gloria Austin

4000 BC   3000 BC   2000 BC   1000 BC   0   1000 AD   PRESENT

FOREWARD

There are more horses in the United States than any other country in the world.

There are greater numbers of breeds of horses in the United States than any other country in the World.

Ironically, the domestic horses in America that initially came from Europe on Columbus' second voyage to the New World was sent back to Europe by the thousands during the First World War.

Originally coming from the Eurasian steppes over 6,000 years ago, the horse's role in warfare, communication, transportation, agriculture, commerce, and industry has been essential in building civilizations around the world and particularly in the United States. Critical for moving people and goods by land, horses historically also provided meat, hair, and leather. Horses are still of great economic importance to the sport and leisure industries. Horses are still valued as working animals in many parts of the world today. The advantage of the horse over cattle, sheep, goats, and all ruminants is that ruminants must rest to digest their food. Horses can break down the cellulose in plant material through hindgut fermentation. This enables them to work all day without the need for digestive rest.

Where are these domesticated horses? Nine countries are estimated as having more than a million horses, with the USA, revealed as having the world's largest population, at 10.150 million. China is next at 6.77 million, and the Americas have three other countries in the "top 5"—Mexico with 6.35 million horses, Brazil with 5.5 million horses, and Argentina with 3.59 million. Other countries with more than a million horses are Mongolia (2.112m), Ethiopia (2.028m), Kazakhstan (1.528m), and the Russian Federation (1.340m).

Figures from the Food and Agriculture Organization (FAO) of the United Nations reveal that the world's equine population has been dropping by about a million horses a year for the three years from 2009 to 2011. Data show there was 60,001,310 horses in 2009; 59,584,428 in 2010; and 58,472,151 in 2011.

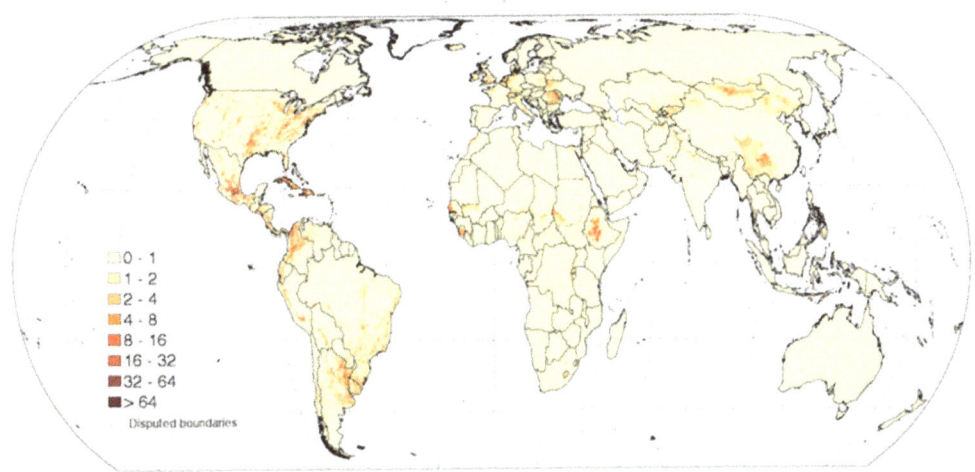

In Rubak Khadka's recent study called "Horse Population, Breeds and Risk Status in the World," various information entities the author researched provided information relevant to the number of different horse breeds in the world. For instance: Oklahoma State University in 2010 reported 217 different horse breeds, while Hall and Rune reported 437 different breeds; The EAAP genetic data bank reported 110 different breeds; the livestock dictionary of Mason reported 592 breeds of horses. Khadka finally concludes that he believes 537 different breeds currently exist in the world.

Remarkably, there is an increase in horse numbers in North America. Horse numbers have shown an increase since 2009, when there were 10.1 million horses, jumping to 10.4 million in 2009, to sit at 10.5 million in 2011. The 2011 figures for individual countries include USA (10,150,000) and Canada (405,000), where an increase of 5000 horses was made from 2010.

Popular breeds in America include Quarter Horse, Paint, Thoroughbred, Standardbred, Tennessee Walker, Arabian, Morgan, Saddlebred, Shetland, Welsh, and Miniature Horse. Of the nine largest breed registries, annual new registrations in Quarter Horses are four times more than the next largest registry.

Many Americans have imported various types of horses, as well. The Gypsy Vanner is an example of a popular horse breed, imported into America.

Memberships in various equine associations suggest that ownership is overwhelmingly female. "Give a woman a horse, truck, and trailer, and she does not want for more." The United States Equestrian Federation organization is 85% female. Some studies say there are 2.9 horses per horse owner (I own four currently.) Many of these women are college-educated, have credit cards, and own their own residence. With the advent of the auto, women's rights, and reproductive freedom, the ownership of horses has changed from men to women.

Throughout history, horses have been costly and beyond the means of most. Kings either levied taxes or used booty from raids to support royal chariots or a cavalry force. Aristocrats also granted land to followers so they could use part of the harvest or taxes to maintain and call into service a warrior class with their own horses. For some, horses are still a symbol of power, wealth, and prestige. Yet today, horses are owned by people from all walks of life.

Today, we horse lovers drive the economy through our horse activities. Men and women work extra jobs to be able to own and enjoy horses.

The nurturing and spiritual connection with the horse has fostered the American connection. Just as Winston Churchill said, "there is something about the outside of a horse that is good for the inside of a man" or woman.

Gloria Austin

INTRODUCTION

Since horses first came to America with the early settlers, they have played a significant role in the history of America. To learn more about the development of horse breeds in the Americas, be sure to read the Equine Heritage Institute book, "Horses of the Americas."

From America's independence to the westward expansion of the country, horses have been a vital part of the history of America.

Of the many horses that George Washington owned, one of his favorites was a horse he called "Nelson." Although Washington is often depicted on a white horse, it was Nelson who is said to have carried the General almost always during the American Revolution. Described as a "splendid charger," the animal stood 16 hands high and was chestnut with a white face and legs. Washington preferred to ride Nelson during the war over his other horse, Blueskin because Nelson was less skittish during cannon fire and the startling sounds of battle. Also, Washington chose to ride Nelson on the day the British army, under the direction of Lord Cornwallis, surrendered at Yorktown, Virginia in 1781. *(cover) (cited from: https://www.mountvernon.org/library/digitalhistory/digital-encyclopedia/article/nelson-horse/)*

Famous people, famous horses, commonplace people, commonplace horses—all have played an integral part in the growth and history of America.

In this modern age, it may be hard to imagine the importance of the horse throughout American history. By the time you finish this book, you will find it hard to believe that we could be where we are today without the horse!

Early Settlers and Explorers

Most people do not realize that the many horse breeds of the Americas that we are familiar with have developed here in only the last 500 years. 500 years ago, there were 60,000,000 bison, thousands of deer, and dogs in North America and llamas in South America. There were no hogs, horses, or cattle; these animals had to come from Europe with the early explorers, early settlers, and colonists.

Throughout the 1500s and 1600s, explorers brought horses with them on their voyages.

Early settlers to the Americas probably assumed the needs for horses would be the same as they had been in Europe—transportation, warfare, and farming. Little did they know that just surviving would be so difficult and that hippophagy (the eating of horse flesh) would be necessary for survival. Until the last years of the 18th century, livestock received a significantly low amount of care. Domestic animals could survive only if they were strong enough to last through the winter, relying mainly on forests and natural meadowland for subsistence. Farmers became more attentive to the well-being of their animals when lucrative markets or sporting opportunities could be gained. As situations improved, more horses survived. Eventually, there were more horses in the Americas than in Europe!

Horses served many purposes in early America.

Hunting

Bounties to protect livestock were usually among the first proclamations in the early colonies. In Plymouth, in 1624, a bounty of two pence was established per wolf "for the incouragement of persons to seeke the destruction of those ravenous creatures." This was changed to five bushels of corn in 1633, a more valuable commodity in the colony. Massachusetts Bay Colony Governor John Winthrop, writing in 1631, noted that the wolves "did much harm to calves and swine between Charles River and Mistic." The town enacted a bounty for wolves in November 1639. By 1641, it was a law in Massachusetts for each man to "look daily after wolf traps." In Rhode Island, Roger Williams enjoined every townsman to rid the area of the "fierce, blood-sucking predators." Williams enlisted  the aid of the Narragansett tribe to rid Aquidneck Island of its wolves. However, the farms of Providence were still under siege. The town officially created a bounty in January 1659, when it was ordered that "whosoever shall from this tyme forward kill any woolves, that they shall have for each woolfe, a halfe penny a head for each head of catell ... provided they kill them within Providence Limetes." The bounties were of considerable profit to some. It was easier for a person on horseback to keep up with the hounds that were used for hunting the wolves, so horses were desirable for hunting. The wolf was the first animal hunted with hounds and horses in Virginia and Maryland. *(cited from: https://www.americanheritage.com/content/fox-hunting-america and http://www.providencejournal.com/opinion/commentary/20140207-robert-a.-geake-when-wolves-ranged-new-england.ece)*

Farming

Four out of five colonists were farmers. Most colonists tilled fields using simple tools such as iron-bladed hoes. Plows were used by those wealthy enough to own horses. It was preferred that horses be at least 14 hands high, but most were smaller. They usually weighed between 600 and 700 pounds. *(cited from: http://www.history.org/Almanack/life/trades/traderural_horses.cfm)*

Transportation and Communication

Horses were the primary mode of transportation. They pulled plows, carts, and wagons. When the colonies in the Northeast were first settled in the early 1600s, the communities lying between Boston and New York were virtually isolated from one another. On January 22, 1673, Governor Francis Lovelace of New York dispatched the first post rider to connect New York and Boston, providing mail service for the settlements. The route taken by this first post rider carried him to New Haven, Hartford, and then Springfield, Massachusetts. The route then followed the "Bay Path," a former Indian trail, on to Boston. This route was known as the Upper Boston Post Road, and the total journey from New York to Boston was some 250 miles. The post rider remained the principal means of communication in colonial America, and his services were not replaced until improved roads permitted stagecoach travel in the late 1700s. The horse provided the means to carry goods to market, to speed people from one city to another, and to bring settlers into the interior of America. Muddy paths gave way to a well-designed road system. The Stagecoach eventually afforded a means of mass transit whereby people could move about in relative safety and comfort *(cited from: http://www.imh.org/exhibits/online/legacy-of-the-horse/colonial-horses/)*

Ranching

After the Spanish arrived in Mexico in 1519, ranches were established and stocked with cattle. Horses were imported from Spain to work on the ranches. When the first Spanish explorers came to the Americas, they brought cattle and cattle-raising expertise with them. Landowners mounted native Indians on well-trained horses and taught them to handle cattle. By the early 1700s, cattle ranching had spread north into what is now Texas, Arizona, and New Mexico and South to Argentina. A variety of regional ranching traditions developed in the Americas. Gauchos are cowboys of the grasslands (or Pampas) of Argentina, Brazil, and Uruguay. In Central Mexico, particularly the state of Jalisco, cowboys are called charros, like the charros from Castile, Spain, who settled the region. In Northern Mexico, wealthy ranchers known as Caballeros employed vaqueros to drive their cattle. Ranching in the western United States are derived from vaquero culture. (cited from: https://www.americancowboy.com/ranch-life-archive/history-vaquero and https://www.nationalgeographic.org/encyclopedia/ranching/)

Commerce

Horses were a profitable commodity, used for trade and export. The soil in New England was not well suited to farming, so horse breeding was economical use of hilly and infertile land. Back when Kentucky was only a remote and unknown woodland, the central horse breeding region of America was Rhode Island. Rhode Island's horse industry got its beginning when John Hull, Treasurer of the Massachusetts Bay Colony, purchased land on the west side of Narragansett Bay from the local Indians. This area was fenced off and set up for horse breeding. At one time, Rhode Island had farms with as many as 1,000 horses. These Rhode Island horses were shipped to all the seacoast colonies. Also, the islands of the Caribbean for use on the plantations. *(cited from: http://www.imh.org/exhibits/online/legacy-of-the-horse/colonial-horses/).*

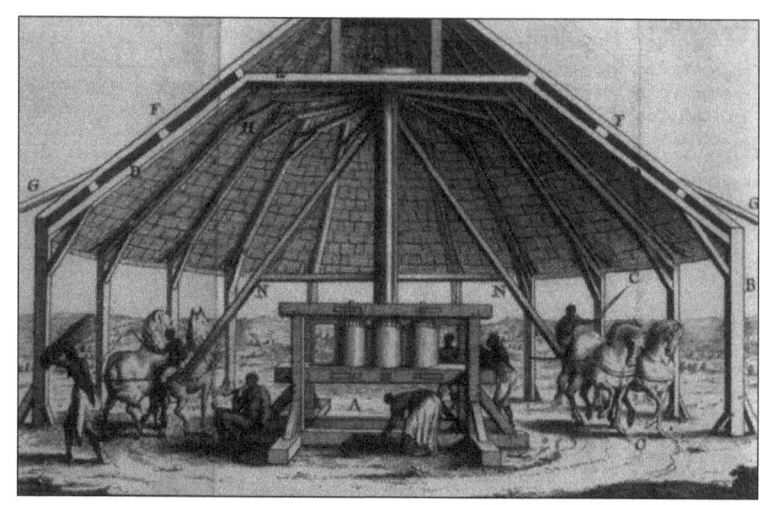

Horse and water powered sugar mills, French West Indies, 1762.

Horses were so abundant in New England that they were exported from New England to the other continental colonies. Beginning in the 1660s and continuing for another hundred years, the primary demand that resulted in the exportation of New England horses came from the sugar plantations in the West Indies. The New England colonies were the accepted source of horses for the sugar islands. This resulted chiefly from the fact that New England was the only ones who possessed a surplus of horses at the time. In most of the other colonies, there was a scarcity of horses. As the settlement of New England grew, it became clear that there were areas that were much better adapted to the raising of livestock than those settled initially. These more favored areas were found mainly in the upper valley of the Connecticut River, along the shore of Long Island Sound and about Narragansett Bay in Rhode Island. Shipping of horses to the islands was a significant source of income to the New England colonies for a hundred years. Between 1771 and 1774, 7,130 horses were shipped from North America to the British Islands. Certain areas were specialized for breeding horses. This was the case, for example, on Fisher's Island, which was given over almost entirely to animal husbandry. Also, in the Connecticut River Valley, the region around Windsor seems to have been another such center. But by far, the most extensive and essential of these specialized areas were to be found in the Narragansett District of Rhode Island. The wealth of the city increased steadily up to the time of the revolution. *(cited from:https://archive.org/stream/horseraisinginco00phil/horseraisinginco00phil_djvu.txt)*

Racing

The very first specially built racetrack in America was constructed in 1665 by New York's colonial governor, Richard Nicholl. Called Newmarket and located in the Hempstead Plains just outside today's border with Queens, it proved an enduring enterprise for colonists. Smaller tracks were soon built in the countryside closer to Manhattan island. Some aristocratic British landowners would even make personal tracks on their estates. The track at Newmarket was "sixteen miles long and four wide, unmarred by stick or stone." *(cited from: http://www.boweryboyshistory.com/2011/05/why-go-to-kentucky-new-yorks.html)*

Rhode Island had a one-mile track at Sandy Neck Beach, South Kingston. Many towns and cities in America have streets called "Race Street." Such roads gained their names from the habit of running horse races on them. In 1674, the citizens of Plymouth, Massachusetts, evidently grew tired or frightened of the races in their villages and created an ordinance forbidding racing.

While horse racing generally followed English rules in the northern American colonies, another form of racing began to flourish in the southern regions. Quarter mile racing was a clear result of the geographical environment. The southeastern seaboard was mostly covered with dense forest. Immense effort was required to clear land, and it was, therefore, precious for agriculture. The racetracks in these wooded regions were sometimes little more than two parallel race paths, ¼ mile in length, cut through the forest. There was a small space at either the beginning of the end of the track. The horses would sometimes be separated by a fence or trees. The quarter-mile track, therefore, gave both the race and the horses their name of "Quarter Horse." Horse racing was the primary form of organized sport in America. Modern towns have athletic rivalries on the football field. In colonial America, town rivalry was centered on horse racing. It was not unusual for the competitors and spectators to travel far to these early quarter-race tracks in the woods and to place considerable wagers on their town's horse. *(cited from: http://www.imh.org/exhibits/online/legacy-of-the-horse/colonial-horses/)*

Conquests

Spanish horses were instrumental in the conquest of the New World. Neither the Aztec nor the Inca had ever seen humans riding animals before; the psychological impact of mounted troops was tremendous. Spanish conquistadors like de Soto were inheritors of some of the finest riding techniques in the whole of Eurasia. The jineta riding style, unique to Spanish cattle-ranchers, emphasized spontaneity, speed, balance in the saddle, and maneuverability. *(cited from: http://www.pbs.org/gunsgermssteel/variables/horses.htm)*

This description of the Conquistadors and their horses is from an actual Aztec account: "The 'stags' came forward, carrying soldiers on their backs. The soldiers wore cotton armor. They bore their leather shields and their iron spears in their hands, but their swords hung down from the necks of the stags. The animals wear many little bells. When they run, the bells make a loud clamor, ringing and reverberating. These animals snort and bellow. They sweat a great deal, and the sweat pours from their bodies in streams. Foam from their muzzles drips onto the ground in fat drops, like a lather of amole (soap). When they run, they make a loud noise, as if stones were raining on the earth. Then the earth is pitted and cracked open wherever their hooves have touched it." *(cited from: http://www.mexconnect.com/articles/682-the-aztecs-speak-an-aztec-account-of-the-conquest-of-mexico)*

Types of Horses in Early America

The horses that were brought and then developed and used in early America were not the types of horses we are familiar with today. Most horses were ambling horses and very small; only 13-14 hands!

Travel was difficult in early America. There were long distances between towns and a lack of roads. The ambling horse was very desirable since it was very comfortable to ride for great distances on uneven terrain. The amble is a method of progressive motion with the same sequence of footfalls as the walk, but in which a hindfoot or a forefoot is lifted from the ground in advance of its fellow hindfoot or its fellow forefoot being placed thereon. The support of the body, therefore, devolves alternately upon a single foot and upon two feet, the single foot being alternately a hindfoot and a forefoot, and the two feet being alternately laterals and diagonals. At no time is the body entirely unsupported.
(cited from: Descriptive Zoopraxograph, 1893, by Eadweard Muybridge)

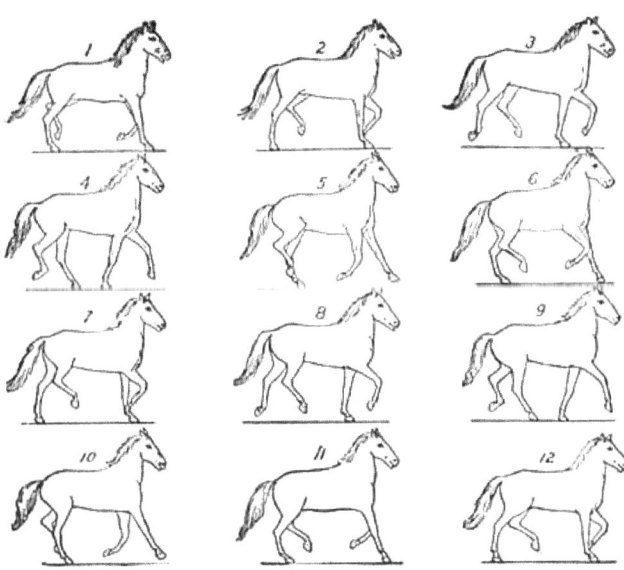

The illustration demonstrates the consecutive foot falls and some characteristic phases of an ambling stride.

Ambling horses are also known as "gaited" horses. There are several 4-beat "ambling" gaits that are approximately the speed of a trot or pace, though smoother to ride. These include the lateral slow gait, rack, running walk, and tölt, as well as the diagonal fox trot. Ambling gaits are often genetic traits in specific breeds, known collectively as gaited horses. In most cases, gaited horses replace the standard trot with one of the ambling gaits.

Ambling gaits are faster than the walk and often the trot, but slower than the canter. Imports of Hobbies from Ireland, along with English Running Horses, were very popular in the Americas due to their speed and comfort. In the Americas, ambling horses were popular at first because there were few roads both in North America and in South America. Travel on uneven and rough terrain was much more comfortable when riding an ambling horse. Ambling gaits are smooth and can be sustained for long periods of time. Ambling horses were particularly desirable in the new America areas where plantation agriculture was practiced, and the inspection of fields and crops necessitated long daily rides. Ambling horses were also popular for transportation and post riders.

The Narragansett Pacer was known as a saddle horse with high endurance. It provided a comfortable ambling gait and was sure-footed. The Narragansett Pacer was swift indeed! He could pace a mile in just over 2 minutes. The British politician Edmund Burke wrote an Account of the European Settlements in America in 1857. In that account, he noted the emerging breeds of horses in New England: "They have, besides, a breed of small horses which are extremely hardy. They pace naturally, though not in a very graceful or easy manner; but with such swiftness, and for so long a continuance, as must appear almost incredible to those who have not experienced it." *(cited from:http://www.newenglandhistoricalsociety.com/ narragansett-pacer-lost-horse-new-england-colonies/*

A Narragansett Pacer

Running horses were very fast gaited horses. Running horses became extinct in England and in Ireland. In America, however, these saddle horse traits have been kept alive. Nowadays, gaited horses are found primarily in the Americas. Genetic research in Ireland by Emmiline Hill and Mims Bower in 2010 and 2012 has discovered a "speed gene" in Thoroughbreds. The speed gene is a "sprint" gene; the speed of today's thoroughbreds originates from the early gaited horses!

In the early Americas, horses existed to serve a purpose, and breeding soon became less haphazard and more purposeful to achieve the needed goal. Before breed registries, horses were organized by breeding practices and performance standards. Rhode Island became the breeding capital of the early North American Colonies.

Ad from the Providence Gazette and Country Journal, January 7, 1764.

The first concern for the early settlers was the size. In the early Americas, many of the horses brought from Europe were small. Settlers soon learned that a larger, more powerful, and more versatile horse was needed. The Dutch horses were over 14 hands, and the English horses were under 13 hands. Stringent regulations were adopted against allowing undersize, colts and stallions to wander as they pleased. To foster quality in American horses, as early as 1668, the court of Massachusetts decreed that only horses "of comely proportions and 14 hands in stature" could graze on town commons. A law was enacted by William Penn in Pennsylvania in 1687, which set a minimum height of 13 hands for free-ranging horses. Any horse more than 18 months old and less than 13 hands had to be gelded. This really did not accomplish what was hoped. It was not until the close of the colonial days when farmers had facilities for breeding stock that there was an increase in the size of the horses. *(cited from: http://www.imh.org/exhibits/online/ legacy-of-the-horse/colonial-horses/)*

Colonial Times

From the very earliest period of New England history, it was customary to allow both horses and cattle to run at large on the public commons. Herds increased in numbers, and settlements became more scattered. Animals began to roam and breed at will and often strayed a considerable distance. Eventually, there were so many horses in the colonies that importations from Europe were no longer necessary. Colonists began to breed horses for their purposes and needs.

In the conflicts with the Indians, horses were of great advantage to the colonists. In both offensive operations and on the frontier where troubles were often imminent, the horse was vital. The possession of horses enabled the settlers to bring aid quickly to one another when attacked and thus saved many an isolated settlement from extinction. That the colonists realized this advantage is apparent from the pains which they took to prevent any horses from coming into the hands of the natives. In several colonies, laws were passed to prevent the selling of any horses to the natives. As late as 1665, it was only after considerable debate that the Plymouth court allowed one such sale to be made to a friendly Indian for purposes of husbandry. *(cited from: https://archive.org/stream/horseraisinginco00phil/horseraisinginco00phil_djvu.txt)*

In early colonial times, horses served to some extent for the draft. Still, for plowing and other heavy work, they were found less serviceable than oxen. The horse's most important use was to furnish a means of rapid transportation from place to place. Before the construction of improved roads, both people and goods moved by horseback, as carriages and wagons could not navigate such areas.

In 1761, Philadelphia, then a significant center of population and wealth, there were only 38 carriages. A packhorse could carry 200 pounds over a long distance. Therefore, individuals moving from one place to another were severely limited in what they could bring with them. The inconvenience involved in travel by horseback added to the slow settlement of America's interior. *(cited from: http://www.imh.org)*

Once roads were constructed, westward expansion commenced in great earnestness. Muddy paths gave way to a well-designed road system. The Stagecoach afforded a means of mass transit whereby people could move about in relative safety and comfort. In all, the 1700s was an age of growth and movement primarily due to the increased use of the horse. The 1700s saw explosive growth in both the quality and quantity of horses. Horses came into high demand. *(cited from: http://www.imh.org)*

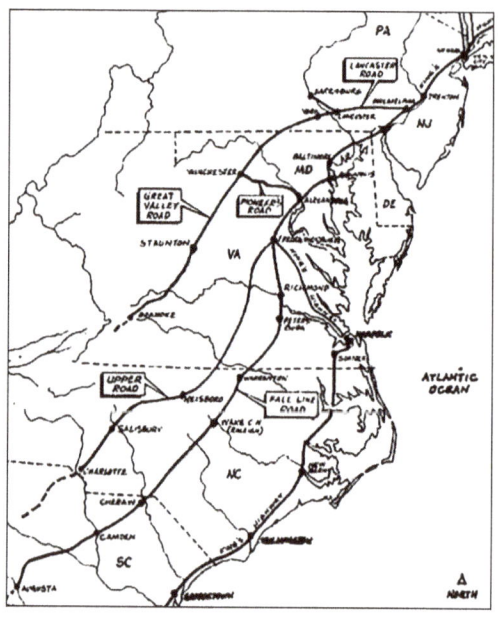

Roads of 1752

Benjamin Franklin was the colonial postmaster general of his majesty's provinces. The noted scientist, philosopher, and irrepressible statesman personally inspected all colonial post offices from Rhode Island to Philadelphia. He devised safer ferry crossings, championed better connecting roads, and measured for milestone markers in his ever diligent and farsighted efforts to unite the colonies. At this time, it took four weeks for a letter from Boston to reach Williamsburg, Virginia. *(cited from: https://www.fhwa.dot.gov/publications/publicroads/02janfeb/exhibition.cfm)*

1763 painting of Franklin in his one-horse chaise, he is receiving an important communiqué from a post rider. His daughter is riding along on horseback.

By 1700, the exportation of horses to the sugar plantations in the British, French, and Dutch West Indies was a well-established part of the trade of New England. This continued an increasing scale during the century that followed. The matter came to a climax in 1731. The British planters presented a petition to Parliament with a draft of a bill that would expressly forbid the continental colonies from selling horses, lumber, and provisions "to any but British subjects." The bill failed but was perhaps a sign of things to come.

Life in the colonies continued to improve; "the British and the colonists were all one big, happy, tea-drinking family." But horses were only owned by the elite for the most part. As elite animals, expensive to maintain, horses did not work in agriculture until the invention of the reaper and other mechanical devices in the nineteenth century. They were present but not plentiful in the colonial period. Philadelphia, for instance, was a compact "walking city," the wealthy used horses for riding, carriage travel, and sport. Most other people walked where they needed to go and hauled goods in handcarts and oxcarts. *(cited from: http://philadelphiaencyclopedia.org/archive/horses/)*

An English newspaper bewails the repeal of the Stamp Act

In 1763, after the Seven Years War, a new generation of British ministers, including Charles Townshend and William Pitt, assumed power. They were convinced that the continued expansion of British trade and political influence depended on the reform of imperial administration and taxation in the North American colonies. Peace on the continent removed the stimulus of a war economy and brought about a recession in the colonies. Debtors in both urban and agricultural sectors experienced the credit squeeze. The balance of trade continued to favor Britain, rendering colonial economies more and more dependent on British commercial ties and financial policy well into the 1770s. Even as colonial standards of living rose, indebted colonists grew increasingly suspicious of British motives and interests. Then along came many acts and taxes. Unlike the Molasses or Sugar Acts, the Stamp Act levied a direct tax on the colonies designed to raise revenue rather than to regulate trade. Colonists considered such measures unconstitutional. Up until now, colonial legislatures had exercised exclusive authority to levy direct revenue taxes in North America, their sovereignty derived directly from the people they represented. By contrast, no colonial representatives sat in the House of Commons. During the debate on the Stamp Act in England, Benjamin Franklin informed British officials that, at minimum, the colonies would need to be represented in Parliament if such taxes were to be imposed. To the British, such demands made little sense. The Stamp Act galvanized colonial society and engendered widespread resistance. It also served as a unifying force among the individual colonies. In 1773, the Tea Act finally ignited the colonists into action. Eventually, in May 1776, the Continental Congress encouraged individual colonies to adopt new governments and formally sever all ties to the English Crown. *(cited from: http://www.taxhistory.org)*

The Horse and the Fight for Freedom

This cartoon, by an unknown artist, demonstrates how Colonial Americans viewed their mother country. They wanted Britain "off their back" and out of the colonies completely. The print - "The Horse of America, Throwing His Master" - depicts a horse, named "America," throwing his rider, King George III. It was initially published in London by William White on August 1, 1779. King George III is depicted as a hapless rider losing control of his mount. The horse "America" looks full of flight and is not taking kindly to the bayonets, swords, and hatchets with which the king is trying to subdue it. *(cited from: https://www.awesomestories.com/asset/view/The-Horse-America-Throwing-His-Master-1779-Cartoon)*

The Use of the Horse in the American Revolution

The rebels had their work cut out for them. They had no government, no money, no army, no navy, no allies, and no game plan. All they had was fiery passion and a few thousand farmers with muskets. Horses were crucial in creating an independent America. The rebel colonists used their own horses in the war. The British often had to steal theirs since it was challenging to ship horses across the rough Atlantic from England. The British were about the horses they took too. One British commanding officer reported that his cavalry troop of some 400 men was, for the most part, mounted on "blooded horses which were quite uniformly kept by gentlemen in Virginia." A major problem that affected the use of Cavalry, both British and American, was forage. It was scarce, difficult to transport, and prevented them from massing their cavalry. Recognizing this, Washington spent a great deal of effort denying the British access to forage. *(cited from: http://www.imh.org and http://www.revolutionarywararchives.org/cavalry.html)*

Before the American Revolution, most military planners believed the American terrain restricted cavalry use. Cavalry was deemed impractical in North America by the planners. There was not any cavalry used during the French and Indian War. A few mounted units did exist, such as the Philadelphia Light Horse, which escorted General George Washington from Philadelphia to Boston, where he accepted the Command of the American Army. This unit was primarily ceremonial and numbered about thirty troopers.

Both sides undervalued the cavalry and did not utilize it. Washington sent home the 400-strong Connecticut "light horse" before the Battle of Long Island. The cavalry used in this battle could have saved New York and possibly shortened the war. It was not until the threat of Banastre Tarleton in the Southern campaigns that cavalry action broke out at a normal military level on both sides.

The troops or companies of light horse raised in the Colony of Connecticut, during the war, were formed into several regiments. Few wore the same dress.

The British cavalry was very effective at intimidating the American infantry. To offset the impact on the morale of his soldiers, General Washington issued the following "General's Orders: The General observed that the army seems unacquainted with the Enemy's Horse; and that when any parties meet with them, they do not oppose them with the same alacrity which they shew in other cases; thinks it necessary to inform the officers and soldiers, that, in such a broken Country, full of Stone-Walls, there is no Enemy more to be despised, as they cannot leave the road; So that any party attacking them may be always sure of doing it to advantage, by taking post in the Woods, by the Roads, or along the stone-walls, where they will not venture to follow them; And as an encouragement to any brave parties, who will endeavor to surprise some of them, the General offers 100 Dollars, for every Trooper, with his Horse and Accoutrements, which shall be brought in, and so in proportion for any part, to be divided according to the Rank and pay of the party. General George Washington," "White Plains, 27 October 1776 *(cited from: http://www.revolutionarywararchives.org/cavalry.html)*

At the outbreak of the Revolutionary War, most of the British troops in the American colonies were billeted in Boston. There was no cavalry, a few field guns, and no field supply system. The shortage of cavalry in the Revolutionary War was a significant drawback for the British. In October 1775, the British undertook a remarkable effort to supply the army in Boston with enough fresh quality provisions to last through the winter. The firm of Mure, Son & Atkinson was contracted to furnish enough fresh food and livestock to fill 36 ships. Only 13 ships eventually made it to Boston. Only the preserved food (sauerkraut, vinegar, and porter, a type of beer) survived intact. Most of the other provisions were rotten or damaged. Out of 856 horses shipped, only 532 survived the voyage. The shipment of many commodities from Britain was deemed impracticable, so the army resorted to local sources for fresh food, fodder, and transportation. This had a significant impact on the course of the war; when supply reserves dropped below the 2-month level, which they often did, British generals stopped thinking about offensive action and began to plan evacuation. To have any hope of victory, the British had to seek out the rebel army and defeat it. Yet far too often, their soldiers were forced to sit and wait or, worse, to evacuate a position, garrison, or city that had already been gained through severe fighting. The effect that logistics deficiencies had on these decisions to wait or pullback is undeniable. The convoy of 36 ships marked the last time that Britain attempted to ship fresh food and livestock to its army. *(cited from: http://www.almc.army.mil/alog/issues/sepoct99/ms409.htm) (above left: "Evacuation Day"—The British leave Boston)*

French cannon at Yorktown by Sidney King

When the British were forced to evacuate Boston, the whole complexion of the war changed. No longer a static siege, General Washington realized that cavalry would be useful in patrolling the Atlantic Coast Line for possible British landings, and to serve as couriers. The horse was a crucial factor in the winning of the revolution fought in the geographic vastness of Colonial America. Despite occupying every major city, the British remained at a disadvantage in the countryside where the use of the horse proved to be a critical element for transport and communication. The kind of warfare employed by the colonists required swift pursuit and withdrawal. The horse was the deciding factor in these types of tactics used to defeat a better organized yet less adaptable enemy.

The speed of the horse made it valuable in delivering messages to political leaders and generals. Long before the telegraph, telephone, and the internet, the horse was the fastest way to deliver a message. At a canter, a horse could travel up to 25-30 mph for short distances and trot up to 8-12 mph over a sustained period. Horses also hauled supplies and armaments. The value of a horse was so high that it was a capital offense to steal one.

Famous Horses and Riders of the Revolution

Since the British fought in a formal European manner, the success of the outnumbered Revolutionaries depended on swift "hit and run" tactics. Their horses provided the means of surprise, and forces under the command of men such as "Light Horse" Harry Lee and Francis Marion contributed significantly to the colonists' victory. The Americans used a very different style of combat that the British called "ungentlemanly." Geography played a big part in the Americans beating the British. In Europe, most of the land was open farmland, which allowed armies to face each other on the battlefield, marching towards the enemy while shooting at each other. The Americans, living in a wilderness, thought that this method of fighting was not practical. The enemies of the colonists were often the Indians. They used guerrilla tactics of striking and then disappearing back into the woods. The Americans picked up this style and used it on their new enemy. In fact, the only army fighting against the British in South Carolina was that of **Francis Marion**, also known as **The Swamp Fox**, along with

Francis Marion, also known as The Swamp Fox

about 50 others. With his uncanny ability to hide in the foliage and pick off the enemy, he was able to terrorize the British and their loyalist allies. Outnumbered 100 to 1, Marion was able to frustrate the British at every step of the way. Using tactics that they had learned to fight the Cherokee; the Swamp Fox became the stuff of legend. Appearing out of nowhere to pick off the enemy and then melt back into the forest like a ghost.

The horse **Paul Revere** rode on April 18th, 1775, was perhaps named **Brown Beauty**. Esther Forbes, Paul Revere's Pulitzer Prize-winning biographer, argues forcibly that the horse that Revere rode from Charlestown to Lexington was a Narragansett Pacer borrowed from Deacon Larkin of Charlestown, but this has been debated. Paul Revere attempted to ride to Concord to warn that the British were coming, but he was captured on the road to Concord. The 15-mile ride was mostly at a walk with an occasional spurring onwards. Henry Wadsworth Longfellow later immortalized Revere by focusing on him—instead of fellow riders **William Dawes** and **Samuel Prescott**.

Paul Revere's Ride, 1775 by Charles G. Bush

Sallie, ridden by **Captain Jack Jouett**, saved Thomas Jefferson and other influential legislators from capture in 1781. On the night of June 3–4, 1781, Jack Jouett rode about forty miles from Louisa County to Charlottesville to warn state officials of the approaching British Army. The British had been threatening Richmond and central Virginia since the spring, and the General Assembly had fled to Charlottesville. On June 3, British cavalry under Lieutenant Colonel Banastre Tarleton assembled in Louisa County to attack Charlottesville. Jouett noticed them, guessed their intentions, and raced ahead to warn Governor Thomas Jefferson and other members of the state government. The assembly escaped to Staunton while Jefferson retreated first to Monticello and then, eventually, to his second home at Poplar Forest, leaving Virginia without an elected governor for a few days. The ride was noted as "probably… the most difficult feat of horsemanship known to history," by one authority at the time.

The American Revolution was a local war, with friends and families on opposite sides, spies next door, and battles right in their neighborhoods. Everyday citizens knew what was at stake and aided the war effort in a multitude of ways, and 16-year-old **Sybil Ludington** was one of these informal soldiers. Her father, Colonel Ludington, had trained his family on how to protect each other and their home.

Sybil Ludington

When a messenger arrived at the Ludington farm on April 26, 1777, too exhausted to travel further, Sybil became the logical choice to ride out and muster the militia. Her father needed to stay at the farm and order the troops as they arrived. British General William Tryon had landed off the coast, moving inland from unopposed. His 2,000 soldiers reached the town of Danbury, Connecticut, and set fire to private homes and the Continental Army storehouses of meat, flour, rice, molasses, uniforms, shoes, and gunpowder, all vital supplies for the colonists' war effort. The message that Danbury was burning was an important one. If Tryon's army continued, they would soon reach the large warehouses at Fredericksburg, potentially crippling the revolutionary movement, or they could attack General George Washington's army two days away at Peekskill. The militia troops had taken a break from months of battle, returning home to plant their spring crops.

Sybil mounted up. She took off through the dark rain, riding from farm to farm on the 40-mile circuit. When she finally reached home at dawn, nearly 400 militiamen had gathered on the Ludington farm. They immediately marched to Danbury, fewer than the British, but with surprise on their side. The British may also have been hindered by consuming the colonists' stores of rum the night before. This became known as the Battle of Ridgefield. The militia joined with Continental Army troops to drive General Tryon's army back to their ships, an instrumental day in preserving the course of the American War of Independence. The militia was able to push the British off Long Island Sound thanks to her quick warning. Often young women and boys were messenger riders because they were light and skilled riders. *(cited from: http://www.equitrekking.com/articles/entry/sybil-ludington-and-her-horse-star-heroes-of-the-american-revolution/)*

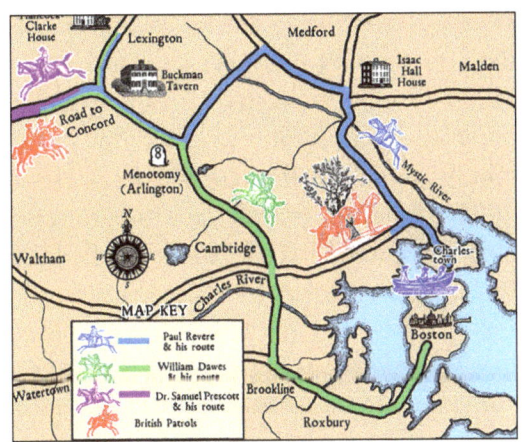

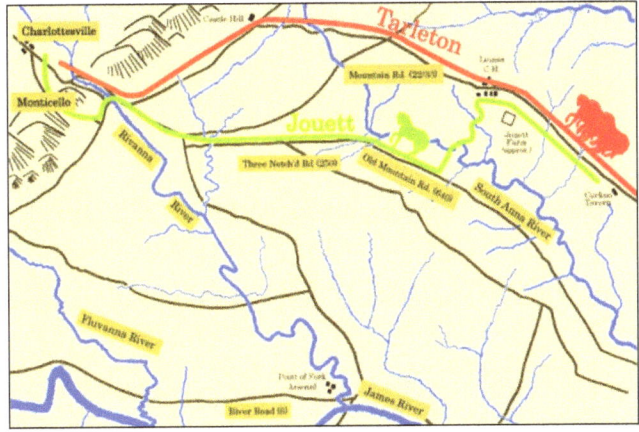

Israel Putnam was outspoken against British taxation policies during the Stamp Act crisis and became active in the Sons of Liberty. His reputation in the French and Indian War secured his appointment as one of four major generals to serve under George Washington. Israel Putnam was most famous for his Bunker Hill heroics. The famous quote, "Don't shoot till you see the whites of their eyes." is credited to Israel Putnam. He was spotted by the British and was being chased down at full gallop. He jumped his horse down a steep rock-stair precipice to escape. The stunned British reined their horses and could do nothing but shoot at him. Although brave, self-confident, and energetic, Putnam was not competent to fill the generalship that his popularity had brought him. After 1777, Washington was forced to withhold important commands from him. *(cited from: https://www.u-s-history.com/pages/h1294.html)*

Israel Putnam

Henry Lee III was a natural cavalryman. He was commissioned as a captain in the fifth group of Virginia Light Dragoons and sent north to join the Continental Army. Leading his men on lightning raids against enemy supply trains, Harry attracted the attention and admiration of General George Washington and was rapidly promoted. In a surprise attack at Paulus Hook, New Jersey, he captured 400 British soldiers with the loss of only one man. His adroit horsemanship soon earned him the nickname "**Light-Horse Harry**." At George Washington's funeral, it was Henry Lee who made the now-famous statement, "First in war, first in peace, and first in the hearts of his countrymen." *(cited from: https://www.thehistorycat-us.com/the-american-revolution and http://www.imh.org and https://www.stratfordhall.org/meet-the-lee-family/henry-lee-iii/)*

Henry Lee III

Despite seeing paintings of **George Washington** most often on a white horse, George Washington's favorite horse was a 16-hand chestnut horse named **Nelson**. Nelson Was a gift from the Governor of Virginia, Thomas Nelson, Jr. Nelson stood his ground better in the heat of battle than his white horse, **Blueskin** (Washington's other mount, named so because of the bluish, black skin under the white hairs of the horse.) Washington was also less noticeable in battle on Nelson than on a white horse.

Nelson was no longer ridden after the war but lived at the stable and paddock at the Mansion House Farm as something of a pampered pet. It was reported that George Washington would walk around the grounds of the estate and stop at Nelson's paddock, when the old warhorse would run, neighing, to the fence, proud to be caressed by the great master's hands. Nelson died in 1790 at age 27 at Mount Vernon.

George Washington on Nelson

George Washington on Blueskin

Most historians agree that if the colonists had not had the fast-striking cavalry, the revolution would have dragged on, perhaps ending in disaster, and dashing the hopes for an independent America. When the war ended, Congress reduced the army to 80 regulars to guard the military supplies stored at West Point. All the cavalry regiments were disbanded.

The Horse and the Advancing Frontier

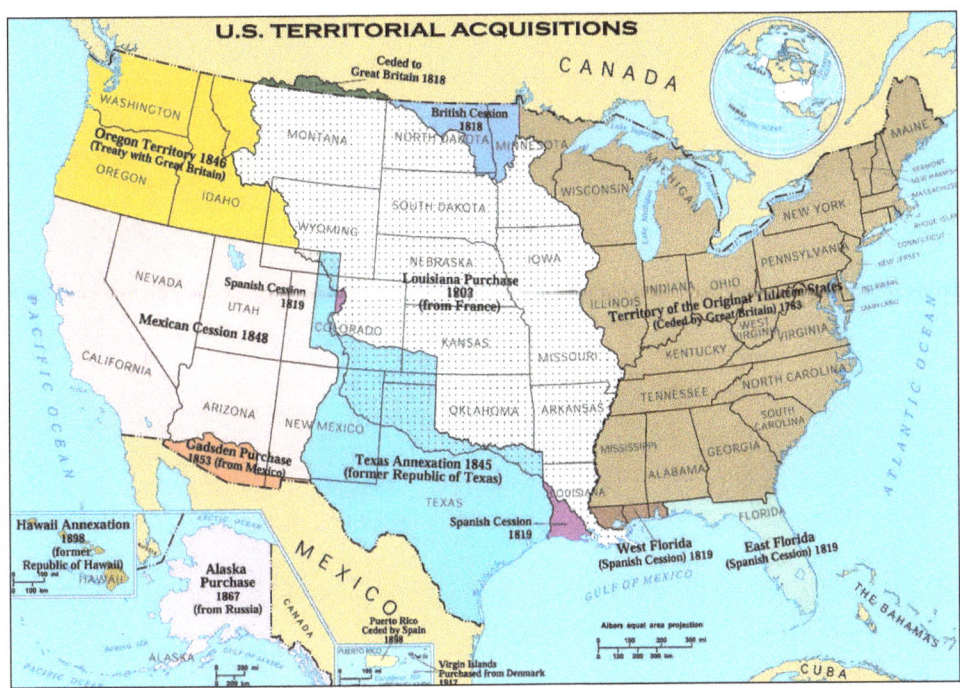

The Wilderness Road

In 1775 Colonel Henderson purchased, from the Cherokees, 20 million acres of land embraced by the Ohio, Kentucky, and Cumberland Rivers. Daniel Boone led the first group of land seekers to the holdings of Colonel Richard Henderson. They started building a fort site, which became Boonseborough. None of these land seekers brought their families with them. In July 1775, when news of fighting at Lexington and Concord reached Boonesborough, most of these land seekers fled back east. In September, Boone returned and, on his trip with 20 other men, he blazed and widened the Wilderness Road. This time he was accompanied by his wife and daughters—the first white women to enter Kentucky. They were the first genuine settlers in Kentucky.

Daniel Boone escorting settlers through the Cumberland Gap by George Caleb Bigham

As Kentucky began to be settled, there were two routes for those who wished to settle there: the Ohio River or the Wilderness Trail. River travel allowed settlers to freight their possessions. However, it was dangerous for two reasons: navigational hazards and British-armed Indians that still controlled the Ohio River Valley. Indian attacks were also a threat to those who chose the overland route. The trail led through territory owned by Virginia and travelers could assemble at frontier stations to form large parties. However, the land route was restricted to pack horses, which necessitated leaving bulky household items behind. As a result, four years after Boone blazed his trail, Virginia authorities addressed the need for the path to be improved for those who wished to establish permanent homes in Kentucky. The transition from Wilderness Trail to Wilderness Road began in the summer of 1780. William McBride of Kentucky County joined forces with John Kinkead of Washington County and improved the trail for horse-drawn wagons to pass. *(cited from: http://kentuckyancestors.org/the-untraveled-history-of-the-wilderness-road/)*

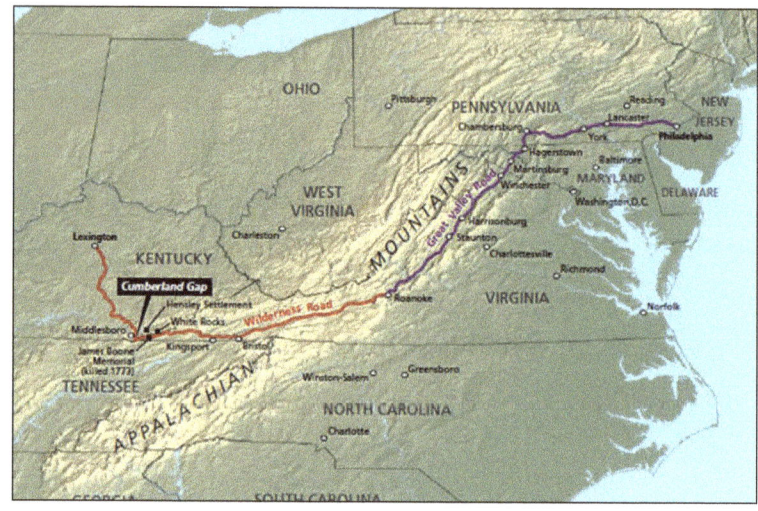

The Wilderness Trail was transformed into a well-marked pathway for pack trains of thousands of settlers. The Wilderness Road would serve as the pathway to the western United States for some 300,000 settlers over the next 35 years. Also, the road provided a route for farm produce, horses, cattle, sheep, and hogs. These were intended for sale in markets closer to the coast. They were also sent west to supply the growing western settlements. In 1792, Kentucky was admitted to the Union as the 15th state.

By 1840, the use of the Wilderness Road had declined. Advances in engineering had enabled waterway travel via the Erie Canal and through the rivers of the Ohio Valley. One segment of the Wilderness Road was among the first roads in the United States to be paved. Later, the old trail would be linked to the famous Dixie Highway that connected Detroit, Michigan, to Miami, Florida.

After the revolution, postwar economic conditions on the seacoast were adverse, so westward expansion gained even further momentum. The Northwest Ordinance, passed by Congress in 1787, further spurred westward immigration. Slowly, the map of a continent-spanning nation was forming.

Lewis and Clark

In 1804 Meriwether Lewis and William Clark led a party across the wilderness acquired by the Louisiana Purchase and through the Oregon Country. Once beyond the Great Falls of Missouri, Lewis became increasingly aware that horses would be the only means of fighting against time and geography, which were racing against him toward another winter. He voiced his worries on July 27th: "We begin to feel considerable anxiety with respect to the Snake Indians. If we do not find them or some other nation who has horses, I fear the successful issue of our voyage will be very doubtful now, several hundred miles within the bosom of this wild and mountainous country." (cited from: http://www.lewis-clark.org/article/3342) In their journeys, they met Toussaint Charbonneau and his Indian wife, Sacagawea. Through Sacagawea, they were able to acquire horses from her brother. He also provided information about the trails to the West. Without the horses, the journey could not have continued. During their 7,689-mile, 28-month journey, they made the first U.S. crossing from the Missouri River to the Pacific coast. Their expedition bolstered the U.S. claim to the Oregon Country, purchased from England 40 years later.

The expedition of Lewis and Clark impacted America's imagination and desire to start a new life in the West, and so the migration west began!

Trailblazers and Mountain Men led the way for covered wagons. Mountain men were trappers and explorers who roamed the North American Rocky Mountains from about 1810 through the 1880s with a peak population in the early 1840s. They were instrumental in opening the various emigrant trails that eventually widened into wagon roads allowing Americans in the East to settle the new territories of the far West. The mountain men and the big fur companies originally opened these routes to serve the mule train based inland fur trade. Eventually organized wagon trains of settlers ventured over these roads to settle the American West.

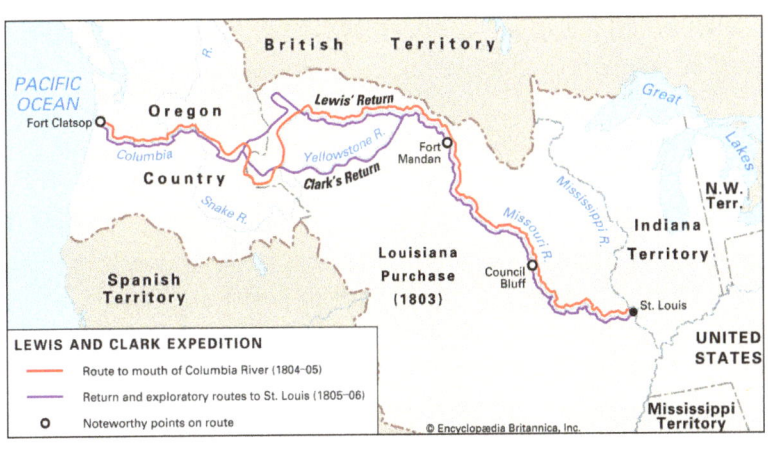

The Impact of Agricultural Inventions

Plows were few - they were costly, and the animal power needed to pull them was limited. Technology had to be improved so that plows might become more cost effective; up to 3 horses or 6 oxen were required to counter the immense friction of poor plow designs. Every agricultural advancement of the time was achieved through plowing, including erosion prevention, and weed reduction. The efficiency of this work was dependent upon the wooden curvature on the furrow side that implemented the separation of the soil after the coulter tip had initially broken the ground. This wooden moldboard needed to be as efficient as the bow of a ship moving through the water, and it was this objective that Thomas Jefferson ultimately achieved. His plow was so light that 2 small horses or mules could pull it with less labor and in less time.

In July 1831, 22-year-old Cyrus McCormick cut 6 acres of grain in one afternoon with his reaper. Before this, it took two to three men an entire day to scythe the quantity of grain that a reaper could cut in a few hours. McCormick's invention gave the farmer an additional power source—the horse.

Cyrus McCormick style reaper

Along with the McCormick hillside plow of 1831 and the Deere steel plow of 1837, these agricultural machines were consequential in agricultural history because they represent the increasing momentum of westward expansion. *(cited from: https://www.farmcollector.com/farm-life/making-american-plow)*

Harrowing a Dakota wheat field.

Bonanza farms were farms of vast acreages created from the sale of land by the Northern Pacific Railroad to its investors to cover its debts. These farms included thousands of acres and produced abundant wheat crops. The absentee landowners hired local managers to run the farms. Through the creation of bonanza farms, Minnesota and North Dakota became one of the country's largest wheat-producing areas. Between 1875 and 1890, bonanza farms became highly profitable using new machinery. *(cited from: http://www.mnhs.org/library/tips/history_topics/62bonanza.php)*

These new tools, along with the creation of larger farms and the expansion of railroads and canals for easier shipment, influenced an agricultural development that led to the need for more horses and mules. The national census of mules in the U.S. in 1860 was 1,129,553. Between 1867 and 1869, the horse population increased by 37%, and mule population by 32%. Between 1900-1910, the national horse population increased by 70%, from 13 million to 23 million.

Gold!

John Charles Fremont was a young army officer known as the Pathfinder. He was married to the daughter of the powerful senator Thomas Hart Benton who was an advocate of transcontinental expansion. In 1842 Fremont was made the head of an expedition to explore the Far West. His exploits made America more aware than ever of the West, especially the Oregon territory. Thousands headed west, and in 1846 Britain recognized America's interests granting the Oregon territory to the U.S.

In 1848 a treaty with Mexico granted California and most of the Southwest to the U.S. for 15 million dollars. On January 24, 1848, gold was discovered in California. Nine days later, California was added to the Union. Thousands of people headed for California. Few struck it rich, but most stayed to farm or start businesses. California's population increased tenfold between 1848 and 1853. The overland 49ers took variations of what became known as the Oregon-California Trail, which wound through what today we call Kansas, Nebraska, Colorado, Wyoming, Idaho, Utah, Oregon, and Nevada. This took the travelers over swamp and river, desert, and mountain. To make it into California, you had to cross the Sierra Nevada Mountains before winter set in. *(cited from: http://www.wondersandmarvels.com/2015/09/why-i-fell-in-love-with-sarah-royce-pioneer-woman-of-the-gold-rush.html)*

It was only 72 years since the colonies declared their independence, and now the nation encompassed a vast continental domain. However, much of it remained to be settled.

Western Expansion - Getting There

Canals were waterways through the wilderness. The Erie Canal was built to bring trade from what was the American West back to the Port of New York. The Erie Canal runs from the Hudson River to Lake Erie, connecting the Great Lakes with the Atlantic Ocean. The entire canal open in 1825. It was the first transportation route faster than carts pulled by draft animals and cut transport costs into, what was then, the wilderness by about 95%.

It resulted in a massive population surge in western New York, opened regions further west to increased settlement, and was a prime factor in the growth of New York City as a port of trade. Canal channels were 4-5 ft deep, and mostly mules pulled the flat bottom scows up and down the canal. Between 1825 and 1900, hundreds of thousands of mules labored on the canal towpaths.

With the development of roads, as bad as they were, came the growth of stagecoach and wagon transportation.

The most common starting point for the journey west was Independence, Missouri. The journey usually began in late April, early May. Often, there were substantial jam ups, as everyone wanted to leave at the same time. Most had grossly overloaded their wagons, and the trail was littered with debris. Horses were not often used to pull the wagons. This task was more often left to mules and oxen. Oxen were easier to handle than mules, maintained condition better, and were cheaper than mules but, they were slow, averaging 2 miles per hour.

Several trails headed to the West.

The Southern Route started at Fort Smith, Arkansas. It traveled south through New Mexico and Arizona then headed north into California, ending in San Francisco.

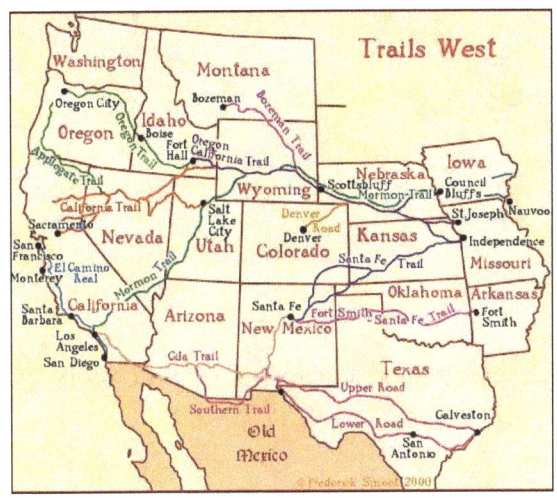

The Santa Fe Trail was the first significant trail. It began as a trade route. It was 800 miles from Independence, Missouri, to Santa Fe, the capital of Spanish New Mexico.

The Oregon Trail was 2,000 miles and originated from Independence, Missouri, and ended in Willamette Valley, Oregon. It was used by Native Americans, Lewis and Clark, fur traders, mountain men, and finally, migrants.

The Mormon Trail was 1,300 miles and started in Nauvoo, Illinois, and ended in Salt Lake City. 16,000 Mormons migrated west between 1847 and 1853.

Due to reports from the explorations of Lieutenant Zebulon Pike and Major Stephen Long, most people considered the Great Plains area of the United States as "The Great American Desert." But in 1847, the Mormons, led by Brigham Young, were seeking a place to leave in peace to practice their religion. On April 5, 1847, they set out. The wagon train contained 73 wagons, 1 cannon, 93 horses, 52 mules, 66 oxen, 19 cows, 17 dogs, and some chickens, and enough supplies to fully provision the group for one year. They settled in the Great Salt Lake valley in Utah. By the early 1850s, church converts in England began booking passage on ships. These ships brought them to St. Louis, Missouri, from there they would journey up the Mississippi and Missouri River to jumping-off locations to travel westward by wagon.

The PEF (Perpetual Emigration Fund) had helped Mormon converts travel by wagon train across the Great Plains to Great Salt Lake City. The premise that those taking advantage of the fund would, in turn, replenish it did not pan out, however, as settlers' reimbursements could not keep up with new emigrants' demands. With declining money and material available for the PEF, in September 1855, Brigham Young fell back on an old plan to make handcarts and let the emigration foot it. Despite the disastrous crossings that were the worst single tragedies to befall any overland travelers, the church continued to support the handcart scheme. From 1857 through 1860, companies of Mormons from Britain and Scandinavia trudged the trail with their two-wheeled carts. Many would die, but the majority of the faithful would reach Utah Territory. In 1896, the territory became the state of Utah. *(cited from: https://truewestmagazine.com/the-mormon-handcart-migration/ and http://www.historynet.com/mormon-handcart-horrors.htm)*

Handcart Pioneers - Converts of the Mormon faith pushing and pulling their laden carts to a new homeland in the valleys of the mountains.

The Prairie Schooner was the vehicle of choice for many migrants heading west. Modeled after the much larger Conestoga Wagon, the Prairie Schooner featured wider wheels for softer surfaces. The cover was treated with linseed oil for waterproofing. Most had added benefits such as a toolbox, water barrel, and a feed trough.

This was dangerous travel for all. Travelers were challenged with disease, injury, broken equipment, supply shortages, and other calamities. There was always the race against early winter snow as well.

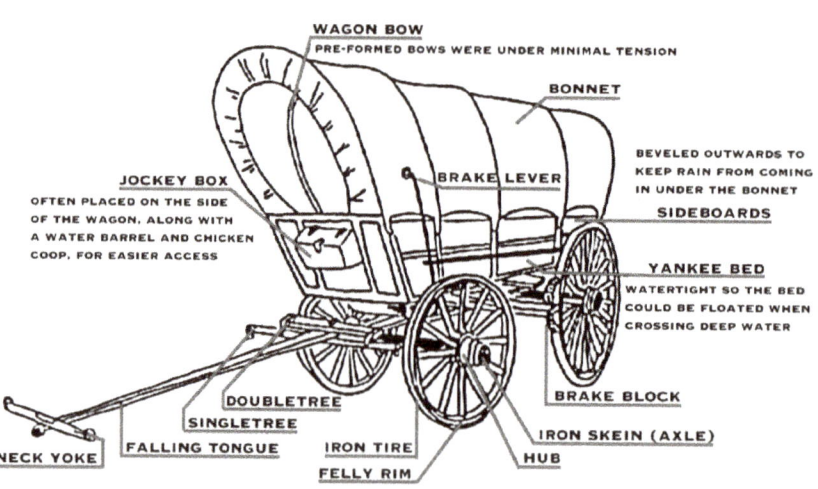

- The canvas top was supported by a frame of bowed wood. The ends could be closed with a drawstring in bad weather.

- Teams of mules or oxen pulled the heavy wagons.

- The wooden wheels were rimmed in iron to prevent wear.

- The wagons were packed full with everything from basic necessities to a family's most treasured possessions. Heavy items often had to be abandoned along the trail.

- Wagons were constructed mostly of wood and with a minimum of metal parts in order to keep them lightweight.

Settling the West

The horse played a vital role in the settling of the great American West.

At first, there were tent cities, and as cities and towns developed, the horse was used for the building of the towns. The horse was used to get supplies to the towns as well.

Transportation

As the West developed, people began to travel from town to town.

Stagecoaches provided regular transportation and communication between St. Louis and San Francisco. The Butterfield Overland Mail received the first contract by the U.S. Postmaster in 1857, and stages began running in 1858 and ran through 1861. It carried passengers and U.S. Mail from Memphis, Tennessee, and St. Louis, Missouri, to San Francisco, California. The route covered about 2,750 miles, and stages made the journey in an average of 20 days. Two runs were made a week. A one-way fare was $200. At the height of success, the company had 800 employees, 139 relay stations, 1,800 head of stock, and 250 Concord Stagecoaches.

Perfected in 1827 by the Abbot Downing Company of New Hampshire, the Concord Coach used an innovative suspension system, called thorough braces, so that the body would rock like a cradle. Concord Coaches were exported all over the world to places that had little or no road systems.

Concord Stagecoach replica commissioned by Gloria Austin

J. Stephens Abbott and Lewis Downing

The Stagecoach was pulled by a team of 6 horses that were changed out every 10 miles. The driver drove a route that was 50-60 miles long. The stage traveled day and night and made periodic stopovers at home stations where passengers were fed - usually rancid bacon, stale bread, and bitter coffee.

The ride was far from "romantic. It was a very bumpy and often harrowing journey. The passengers had little or no sleep, and the food was terrible. It was dusty with either unbearable heat or freezing temperatures. The only consolation was the beautiful scenery.

THE AMERICAN HORSE - THE IMPORTANCE OF THE HORSE THROUGHOUT AMERICAN HISTORY

Communication

As cities and towns developed, there was a need for timely communication between the settlements. The Pony Express operated from April 3, 1860, to October 24, 1861. It was founded, owned, and operated by the freighting firm of William H. Russell, Alexander Majors and William B. Waddell. The purpose was to provide a faster mail delivery service between St. Joseph, Missouri and Sacramento, California. Their reason for establishing the Pony Express was to prove that the central route was viable all year long and to obtain the government mail contracts. At the brink of the Civil War, California was thought to be thinking about secession, so communication with the East was crucial. Though the Government made many false promises to the founders, they believed that the Pony Express should keep on running. Russell, Majors, and Waddell felt their obligation to their country and kept it running without regard to their own sacrifice and loss. They assured that California and her gold would remain in the Union. *(cited from: https://nationalponyexpress.org/historic-pony-express-trail/founders/)*

Some 183 men rode for The Pony Express. Riders' ages ranged from 11 to 40, with the average age being around 20 years old. Approximately. 400 horses were purchased to stock the express route. Common breeds were Mustangs, Thoroughbreds, Pintos, and Morgans. The average horse was 14.2 hands, and a weighed 900 pounds.

Riders rode one horse for 10-15 miles and then changed out for a fresh mount. Each rider rode about a 75-100 mile stretch until relieved by a new rider. Overall, the route was around 2,000 miles and took about 10 days. The cost was $5 per half an ounce in the beginning, and eventually, the price was $1 per half an ounce towards the end. The riders carried a "Mochila" or mail pouch. Each corner had a lockable pocket, and it held 20 pounds of mail.

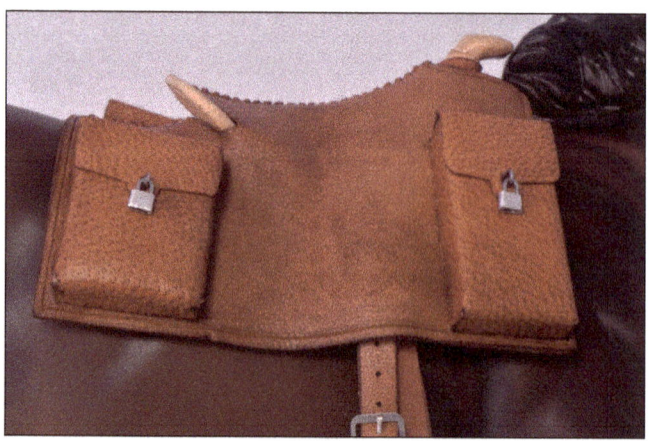

Mochila, spanish for backpack. A mail pouch that overlaid the horse's saddle and held in place by the rider.

The Pony Express captured the hearts and imaginations of people all over the world. It had a short life due to the completion of the telegraph and financial problems. The Pony Express improved east-west communications and proved a central route could be traveled in the winter. The central route supported the idea of building a transcontinental railroad.

Ranching

After the Civil War, there was a shortage of beef in the North; this started a beef bonanza. Large ranches began to develop in the West. Cattle were rounded up from the ranches and driven North to the nearest railways. Cow towns developed in Sedalia, Abilene, and Kansas City.

Often, 3,000 head of cattle needed to be driven by contract drovers on cattle drives to the "cow towns." The cattle drive covered between 10-15 miles a day, and overall the trip took about 6 weeks. The Scout usually rode half of a day ahead of the herd, followed by chuckwagons that led the way to suitable campsites.

It took six men per 1000 head of cattle. Most of these "cowboys" were boys ages 12-18. They signed on for a rate of $25-$40 a month. Unlike the movies, they rarely carried a gun. Cowboys worked with cattle and were excellent riders who knew how to rope. The Trail Bosses were usually in their 20s; they kept records, gave orders, and supervised on the drive. The Ramrod was the person who made sure everything was in order and followed the Trail Boss' directions. The Drag Riders followed behind the herd and were usually the least experienced riders. The Swing Riders helped push and make sure the cattle turned the right way. The Pointer led where to go and rode at the front of the herd. The Cook drove the chuck wagon and was usually an old or previously injured cowboy.

The Chuck Wagon served as the center of life. A rancher, named Charles Goodnight converted an army supply wagon into the first "chuckwagon." The Cook served as not only the cook but was the barber, doctor, banker, mediator, or any other duty that was required. The wagon was typically pulled by teams of 4 horses or mules.

The destination was the stockyards in the "cow towns."

With the invention of barbed wire in 1874, ranchers contained their cattle in smaller grazing areas with water. Homesteaders would cut the barbed wire due to being cut off from water supplies. The fight for land was on! Eventually, the wind pump was invented. This device used the strong winds on the plains to pump water from underground so that farms and ranches could be sited anywhere, rather than being near water.

The period 1880-1885 was the peak of ranching on the plains. Livestock was a sure way of making money. As cattle prices rose, cattle ranchers put more and more animals on the open range. This puts pressure on the amount of available grazing land. The drought of 1883 added to this problem. At the same time, the demand for beef in the East began to fall, so the prices paid for cattle fell. Since prices were falling, the ranchers kept their cattle on the range instead of sending them for slaughter, which added to the problem of finding enough grazing land. Then came the final blow. The winter of 1886-87 was especially severe. Thousands of cattle died in the icy blizzards and freezing cold; 15% of the herds died. It became more sensible to create smaller quantities of better-quality beef.

Mining

Donkeys, mules, and horses were used as pack animals above ground and used as draft animals underground.

Horses and mules were also used to supply the mines and mining towns. In 1866 in Virginia City, Montana, there were 2,500 men, 3,000 teams, and 20,000 oxen and mules hauling supplies from Fort Benton.

In addition to the gold mines, there were many inland silver and copper mines. Large mule trains hauled the gold, silver, and copper out of the mines. *(cited from: Gold Rushes and Mining Camps of the Early American West, p. 134)*

Farming

In 1862 the U.S. Congress passed the Homestead Act. This law permitted any 21-year-old citizen or immigrant intending to become a citizen to lay claim to 160 acres of land known as the Great American Prairie. After paying a filing fee, farming the land, and living on it for five years, the ownership of the property passed to the homesteader. People came from all over the world to take advantage of this opportunity. By 1900 over 600,000 claims had been filed. Different areas of land were opened for homesteading at different times. This often-created land rushes where people would race in to claim the best plots of land.

Oklahoma land rush

Homesteaders faced many challenges. Everything about the prairie was extreme. The land was flat and treeless, and the sky seemed to go on forever. On a tall-grass prairie, the grass sometimes grew to be more than six feet tall. It is said that riders on horseback could pick wildflowers without dismounting.

Home built with sod.

Women worried about their children getting hopelessly lost in the grass. Summer brought endless days of heat when the surface temperature could exceed 120 degrees. Periods of drought, rainstorms, tornadoes, swarms of grasshoppers that could destroy fields of crops, and never-ending wind also challenged settlers. Winters were long and cold. Blizzards were so intense that they could trap livestock and homesteaders under the snow. During the long winter of 1886, horses and cattle died when their breath froze over the ends of their noses, making it impossible for them to breathe.

Building a home—sometimes of sod - and establishing a farm was a challenge for even the most experienced farmers. Still, the free land, abundant wildlife, and richness of the soil made the trial hard to resist. *(cited from: http://amhistory.si.edu/ourstory/activities/sodhouse/more.html)*

Thousands of women took advantage of the Homestead Act that offered free land in the American Great Plains. Women who were single, widowed, divorced, or deserted were eligible to acquire 160 acres of federal land in their own name. A married woman was not allowed to take land in her own name unless she was considered the head of the household. Most homesteading women were young, at least twenty-one, single, and interested in adventure and the possibility of economic gain. *(cited from: http://plainshumanities.unl.edu/encyclopedia/doc/egp.gen.040)*

Horses were essential to the livelihood of the farmer, so horse theft was a serious offense. A horse was a person's transportation and, in the case of a farm animal, a source of income. As the United States was in its growth stages, horse thieves flourished in the frontier areas of the country. A thief could steal a horse and hurry him across state lines or into the Indian territories where local authorities could not easily follow. It was easy, and it was lucrative. Major David McKee of Clark County, Missouri, and a group of his friends formed The Anti-Horse Theft Association (AHTA) in 1853 to combat the problem. There was one major unforeseen problem with their organization. With the advent of the American Civil War, most of the members, including Major McKee, enlisted in the army. Thievery only got worse with the chaos of the war. Rogues became more reckless and desperate—especially with stealing horses and cattle. The AHTA was not a group of vigilantes, who would chase after horse thieves, catch them, and hang them from the nearest tree. They did dole out justice, not from a limb of a tree, but through the courts. The group believed in supporting and upholding the law, and the last thing they wanted to do was break the law. Instead, they worked hand in hand with law enforcement, gathered evidence, and testified in court to punish horse thieves and other criminals. This is probably why the organization grew so large. It was a way for law-abiding citizens to bring order into their lives by working with law enforcement rather than becoming helpless victims. The organization was very active.

Elinore P. Stewart plowing the field, 1913

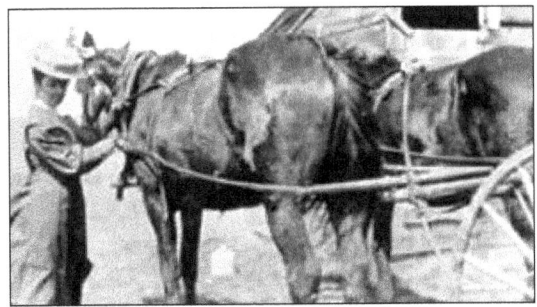

Agnes Lamb on the day she filed on her homestead land near the town of Washburn North Dakota, ca. 1906

33rd Annual Meeting of AHTA of Kansas in 1914. The years before WWI saw the peak membership of the organization. Nationally the membership was 43,000 - Kansas, Missouri, and Oklahoma had strong chapters.

It is stated that from 1899 to 1909, the Oklahoma AHTA recovered stolen horses and other livestock valued at $83,000. Four hundred suspected thieves were caught, and 272 of them were convicted. That was just in the state of Oklahoma. *(cited from: http://www.lrgaf.org/articles/ahta.htm)*

Suborder 300 of the AHTA: Springfield, Missouri 1900-1910 by Duncan Studios.

This is the constitution and bylaws of the Kansas Division of the Anti-Horse Thief Association. The group was first organized to suppress plundering during the Civil War. Later it broadened its charter to "aid in the upholding of civil laws, to ensure the safety of our people, and the security of our property against loss by thieves, robbers, murderers, vagrants, tramps, incendiaries and all violators of the law."

Railroads

The building of the railroads was one of the most significant engineering feats of the 19th century. At any one time, 10,000 animals and 8,000–10,000 laborers were working on the construction. The growth of the railroads brought more people; more people needed more horses! Horses were needed for transportation and farming and building the railroads!

Native Americans

Native Americans were first introduced to the horse by the Spaniards, who brought them from Europe in the 1600s. They obtained the horses by stealing them or trading for them. The Native American's use of the horse spread throughout the plains.

The horse transformed the Plains Indian's world from marginal hunters and farmers to nomadic and proud warriors. The horse created a better lifestyle for Native Americans by providing them with unprecedented mobility for moving camp, hunting, trading, and warfare.

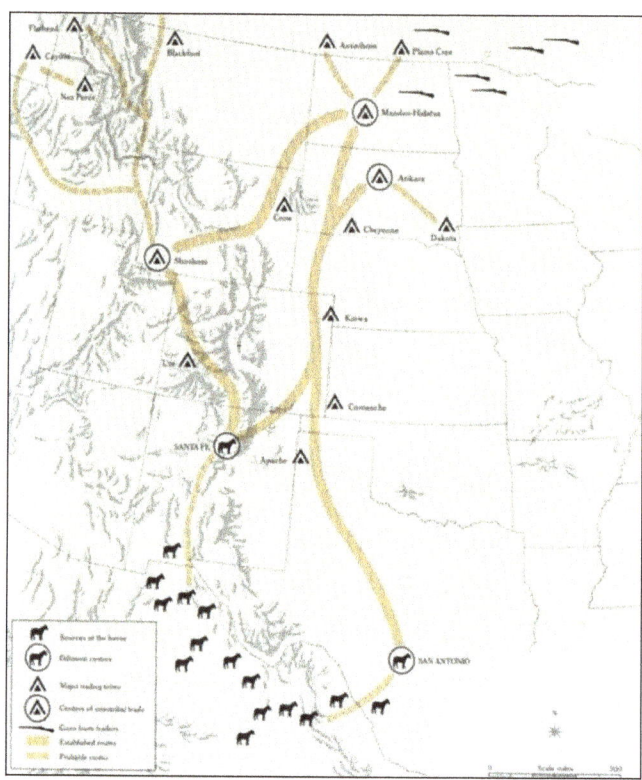

The Aura of the West

Back in the East, books and newspaper reports described life in the West as an exciting adventure inspiring more people to head West. The phrase, "Go West Young Man," was often credited to the American author and newspaper editor Horace Greeley. But nothing inspired people to head West more than the Wild West Shows!

Wild West shows were traveling vaudeville performances in the United States and Europe. In 1872 the legendary plainsman, Wild Bill Hickok, joined several cowboys and Indians in a "Grand Buffalo Hunt" staged at Niagara Falls and on May 19, 1883, William F. "Buffalo Bill" Cody opened Buffalo Bill's Wild West show in Omaha, Nebraska; this was the first and prototypical Wild West show lasting until 1913.

Civil War

The Use of the Horse in the American Civil War

The Civil War (1861-1865) was a defining event in the development of American history. After the Civil War, America experienced rapid urban industrial growth. For the first time in American history, municipal and industrial forces were winning out over the agricultural traditions of American life. The role of the horse was beginning to change.

The Civil War was one of the earliest modern wars. The application of improved and increasingly modernized weaponry to the battlefield. New technology like repeating rifles, breech-loading weapons, and the rapid-fire Gatling gun contributed significantly to the war's status as America's most deadly war. The Civil War demanded recruitment and mobilization of both animals and people on an unprecedented scale

The Civil War was a war powered by equines. Rather than reduce the reliance on horses and mules, industrialization produced the methods and need for horsepower on a bigger scale more than ever before. The acquisition, as well as care of horses for the war, required an enormous amount of organization and effort. Horses were one of the most significant expenditures of the war budget. The purchase of the horse was only part of the expense; without training, feed, shoes, proper fitting tack, and regular maintenance, horses became unusable for military service.

At the start of the Civil War, the Northern states held approximately 3.4 million horses, while there were 1.7 million in the Confederate states. The border states of Missouri and Kentucky had an additional 800,000 horses. Also, there were 100,000 mules in the North, 800,000 in the seceding states, and 200,000 in Kentucky and Missouri. Throughout the war, horses and mules perished at rates as astonishing as the human death toll.

Dead horses at Trostle Farm during Battle of Gettysburg on July 2, 1863.

Historians estimate 1.5 million horses and mules died during their wartime service. An estimated 3 million equines participated in the war effort, a figure 36% greater than the number of soldiers populating the northern and southern armies. Approximately 50% of the mules and horses drafted into the war did not survive. *(cited from: http://ushistoryscene.com/article/civilwaranimals/)*

Horses were valuable to the army and to the overall success of military victory, and by late 1864 a prized cavalry mount was valued more than $3,000. $3,000 in 1864 is equivalent in purchasing power to about $58,046 in 2020! The horse population in the nation had significantly been depleted as the war was ending. Horses died in great numbers from disease and exhaustion and made for large targets on the battlefield. Soldiers preferred to shoot horses rather than the enemy because by removing the horse, the cavalry could not advance, and artillery and much-needed supplies could not be hauled.

Most Civil War battles were fought in the South, and it resulted in the confiscation of horses, mules, and donkeys from Southern farmers who relied on the equines for their livelihood. The once vast supply of horses in the United States was greatly diminished by late 1863, causing a single horse to be considered more valuable than a soldier. While men were still plentiful in the North, attrition had decimated its horse population. The Shenandoah Valley Campaigns of 1864 placed an additional strain on an already depleted supply of horses. General Phil Sheridan, for example, required 150 mounts per day during his chapter in the campaign alone. By 1864 the Union Army relied heavily on prized horses in the South to replace the 500 horses it needed daily to sustain its army in the field. *(cited from: http://www.thomaslegion.net/americancivilwar/totalcivilwarhorseskilled.html)*

Civil Warhorses and mules primarily served in three sectors: artillery, cavalry, and supply. The Horse Artillery differed from other light artillery (also known as "mounted" artillery) in that each member of the unit traveled on his own horse. Traditional light artillery had a practice of only some soldiers riding horses. In contrast, others rode on the limbers and caissons, with still others traveling on foot. With each man on his own horse, the unit could move faster and more efficiently. It was the brainchild of Brigadier General William Farquhar Barry, Chief of Artillery for the Army of the Potomac, in 1861. With such a large percentage of the U.S. Horse Artillery being artillery batteries from the regular U.S. Army, it developed a superb reputation for military efficiency, the accuracy of fire, and command presence in the field and in battle. The horses of the battery had to be fed each day, whether the battery moved or not. During the Civil War, an artillery battery might sit in the same place for weeks at a time, and yet consume thousands of pounds of hay and grain each day. Water for the horses was a problem that demanded an adequate solution every day. While in camp, a battery would discover the nearest creek or pond and routinely water the horses there. On the march, water had to be found at the end of each day. If the water was any distance, as it often was, the timing of the watering was critical. The guns were immobile if the horses were absent. *(cited from: http://www.thomaslegion.net/americancivilwar/totalcivilwarhorseskilled.html)*

The role of the cavalry at the beginning of the Civil War was minimal. Horsemen of both armies were initially limited to patrolling and scouting, guarding supply trains and railroads, and providing escorts to generals. The cavalry's military role had dramatically changed by 1863, and the armies were making use of their horse soldiers in more combat situations. Cavalry divisions were utilized by commanders as advance scouts and as a mobile fighting force. These new strategies culminated in the most massive cavalry battle of the war fought on June 9, 1863, at Brandy Station, Virginia. Brandy Station was the opening clash of the Gettysburg Campaign.

Cavalry was dependent on fast movement, so a cavalryman's priority was the care of his horse. Each cavalry regiment had a blacksmith who shod and cared for the animals in camp. On an active campaign, a trooper had to look out for his own animal and care for it. If the horse was disabled, it was easier for a northern soldier to get a new mount from the herd which usually accompanied the army. Southerners brought their own mounts with them into service and woe be to the man whose horse pulled up lame or was injured. It sometimes meant the Trooper became a foot soldier until another horse could be obtained. *(cited from: http://www.civilwar.com/overview/315-weapons/148532-cavalry-62478.html)*

Union army wagon train halted and guarded from Confederate cavalry near Brandy Station, VA, in May 1863

A supply train's journey was one of imminent danger. Both armies were in dire need of provisions, and the capture of a wagon train was as good fortune as a victory in a battle. To protect this train from a desperate dash of the Confederate cavalry, it was "parked" on the outskirts of a forest that shielded it from envious eyes and guarded by the Union lines. One of Mr. Brady's cameras took this photograph during this critical moment. It shows but 1 division of 1 crop. The supply trains of the vast armies numbered thousands of 6-mule teams, and during the march, the wagon train would stretch for several miles. Sherman's supply train consisted of over 5,000 wagons, 800 ambulances, 28,000 horses, and 32,000 mules. His supply train stretched for miles, as did many supply trains that served the Northern regiments.

The supply train was a vital lifeline for the army. Filled with food, clothing, medicine, munitions, and other critical provisions. Trains were also essential but crippled by scarce routes. Although trains would often move much-needed ammunition rapidly near the front, it was the mule and horse that often hauled it to the exhausted troops. The equines of the conflict, too, needed adequate provisions. *(cited from: http://www.thomaslegion.net/americancivilwar/totalcivilwarhorseskilled.html)*

In the South, supply systems soon broke down. The South did not have the iron it needed to repair damaged railroad tracks, so it was left to wagon trains to haul supplies. When wagons broke down, the South did not always have the material they needed to fix them. As the war continued, the shortage of wagons and of horses became ever more severe—this left military commander with starving Confederate soldiers and starving Union prisoners. Rebel forces began stealing from farms in the South, in some cases, leaving nothing for the farmer's family to eat. *(cited from: https://civilwar.mrdonn.org/supplytrains.html)*

During Reconstruction, many soldiers, burdened with battle scars and disabilities, returned to their farms only to find them overrun by trees and brush caused by neglect or abandonment. Other veterans arrived at the homestead only to receive the news that their former livelihoods of farms and fields had been sold by wives and family members to purchase necessities for the harsh winters that had confronted them. In the absence of husbands, fathers, and brothers who had marched to the drums of war, many wives and children had indeed tended the fields, usually with limited success. Still, it quickly vanished as the remaining horses and mules were requisitioned by a nearby army for the war effort. Left to starvation, while adjacent fields were overrun with brush or sell everything to survive was often reality and not a choice. If abandoned fields and appropriated equines were not enough to entertain thoughts of despair, then the local banker or some creditor usually confiscated what remained to compensate for debt or monies owed. Those who had some tillable land remaining were the exception and not the rule. Life can be hard sometimes, but as one soldier who had served and fought for the duration of the Civil War said, "We made it through the war, so we can make it through anything." *(cited from: http://www.thomaslegion.net/americancivilwar/totalcivilwarhorseskilled.html)*

Ruins of Mrs. Judith Henry's House
Bull Run, VA, March 1862
(cited from: http://www.civil-war.net/cw_images/files/images/367.jpg)

Famous Horses and Riders of the Civil War

LITTLE SORREL (ca. 1850 -1886) was a small chestnut gelding ridden by General Thomas Jonathan "Stonewall" Jackson. He was a pacer and had the conformation of a pacer. He survived many fierce battles. Jackson was riding Little Sorrel when he was mortally wounded by friendly fire at Chancellorsville.

Confederate forces had seized a group of Union horses from a Baltimore and Ohio train headed East. Jackson declared them to be Confederate government property. He bought 2 for his own use: Big Sorrel and Fancy for his wife.

After discovering that Fancy had a better temperament for battle and a smooth pace, he took Fancy for himself, renaming him Little Sorrel, his pace was so smooth that Jackson often fell asleep on long marches. Some believe Little Sorrel was a Morgan horse — a favorite of the U.S. Cavalry, prized for their agility, endurance, and low maintenance.

OLD BALDY (1852-1882) was a bright Chestnut with white socks and a white face. He was the horse of General George Meade. Baldy was wounded at least 5 times in battle, and some say up to 14 times. He was raised on the Western Frontier and was initially owned by General David Hunter, under whom he was wounded several times. He was sent to the Cavalry Depot to recuperate, after which General George Meade purchased him for $150. Baldy outlived Meade and served as the riderless horse in Meade's funeral procession in November 1872. He lived another ten years.

WINCHESTER (aka Rienzi) (ca. 1858-1878) was General Philip Sheridan's horse. He was a jet-black stallion with 3 white socks. Winchester / Rienzi was foaled in Grand Rapids, Michigan. His bloodline included Morgan horses of the prestigious Black Hawk line. He had a long stride and walked at roughly 5 mph. At more than 16 hands high, he was significant for the slightly built General Sheridan. Sheridan rode Winchester/ Rienzi almost continuously for the next 3 years — through 45 engagements, 19 fierce battles, and cavalry raids. Winchester/ Rienzi became a national celebrity in October 1864 when he played a role in saving the Union Army from defeat at Cedar
Creek. Sheridan was in Washington DC for a staff meeting, when Confederates launched a surprise attack on his troops in Cedar Creek, Virginia. Sheridan was still 20 miles away in Winchester when he awoke to the sound of cannons. Sheridan rode Rienzi at full gallop towards his troops arriving in time to rally his soldiers: "Men, by God, we'll whip them yet!" he shouted. Sheridan's troops rallied and prevailed, and the dramatic ride created a media frenzy and inspired paintings, prints, songs, and poems. Henceforth, Rienzi became nationally known as Winchester.

TRAVELLER (1857- 1871) was the primary horse of General Robert E. Lee. He was a 16 hand, dappled, iron-grey gelding with black points. Traveller was thought to be at least one-half thoroughbred. He was the son of Grey Eagle, a prominent thoroughbred four-mile racehorse, who sired both Saddlebreds and racehorses. His dam, Flora, was a gaited Kentucky mare. Traveller carried Lee throughout the war, all the way to Appomattox. He was known for his speed, strength, and courage in combat. Every soldier, both Confederate, and Union, knew him by sight. After the War, Traveller remained with Lee and spent his years at Washington College. When Lee died in 1870, Traveller
walked behind the caisson, draped in black crepe. Traveller died a year after Lee in 1871.

CINCINNATI (ca. 1860-1878) (right) was a chestnut stallion, thoroughbred. He was the most famous of General Ulysses S. Grant's horses. Cincinnati was the son of Lexington, the fastest 4-miler in the country (7:19 3/4 minutes). He was 17 hands high and the grandson of the famous racehorse Boston. Cincinnati was given as a present to Grant by an admirer. After the battle of Chattanooga, Grant was in St. Louis, and he received a letter from an S.S. Grant summoning him to his sickbed. The ailing man gave the valuable horse to Ulysses with the stipulation that he must promise that neither he nor anyone else would ever mistreat the horse. Grant thought Cincinnati was the "finest horse he had ever seen." At one point, Grant was offered $10,000 for Cincinnati, and he turned it down. Cincinnati became Grant's favorite horse, and he rarely permitted anyone else to ride him except for Grants'; boyhood friend, Admiral Daniel Ammen, and President Lincoln. Grant allowed Lincoln to ride Cincinnati every day in the last weeks of his life. Of course, he did not know those were his last weeks. Grant found Cincinnati to be gentle and quiet until he was ridden in battle, during which he was full of spirit. He rode Cincinnati to the surrender at the Appomattox Court House. The pair remained together until old age dictated that it was time for Cincinnati to have a good rest, and he was sent to Admiral Daniel Ammen's farm in Maryland, where he later died of old age. *(cited from: https://www.civilwarhorses.net)*

The Growth of Cities

Between 1880 and 1900, cities in the United States grew at a dramatic rate. Owing most of their population growth to the expansion of industry, U.S. cities grew by about 15 million people in the 2 decades before 1900. Many of those who helped account for the population growth of cities were immigrants arriving from around the world. A steady stream of people from rural America also migrated to the cities during this period. Between 1880 and 1890, almost 40 percent of the townships in the United States lost population because of migration. Industrial expansion and population growth radically changed the face of the nation's cities. *(cited from: http://www.loc.gov/teachers/classroommaterials/ presentationsandactivities/presentations/timeline/riseind/city/)*

American horse population peaked at 25 million in 1915. The mule population reached a peak of 6 million in 1925, with mules being used primarily in the South.

In the cities, the horse was indispensable for the movement of people and freight. The many horses were housed in city stables - some 5 stories high! The C. W. Miller Stable erected in 1894 in Buffalo, New York, is still standing and is on the National Register of Historic Places. It is being converted into a school.

The horses were, in turn, dependent on a vast complex of human resources. Teamsters, hostlers, grooms, farriers, blacksmiths, veterinarians, wheelwrights, carriage builders, draymen, liverymen, makers of saddles, harnesses, whips, and other horse accouterments, as well as manure transporters and rendering workers, were all needed to keep the cities moving. Also, hay and oats were raised in a grain belt surrounding each city. The horse trade itself moved thousands of horses from the farms where they were raised; roughly one-tenth were sent to cities with the rest going to industrial or other users. *(cited from: "Where Have All the Horses Gone," pp. 8-9)*

Smith Worthington Saddlery Company produced saddles at a rate of 25,000 every five months. W. H. Wilkins produced over $1,500,000 worth of harnesses and saddles for the Civil War. In 1873 Abbott and Downing employed 275 men in shops that covered 6 acres in Concord, New Hampshire. They produced Concord Coaches that cost $1.00 per pound. The United States census for 1870 reported 7,607 harness businesses operating throughout the country, employing 23,557 harness makers. Of the 258 industries listed, harness making, and saddlery ranked 34th in the number of people employed.

Horse Harness & Saddle Maker Bench – Stitching Horse 1892

John Yenni Harness Maker

J.R. Hewitt Harness Maker

Horse Relics Still Found in Cities

The commerce and transportation of modern cities initially relied on the horse. A city powered by horses needed shelters for them to rest and sleep. In just New York City, there were around 4,500 stables by the beginning of the 20th century. Where did people in the cities get their horses and carriages? The Van Tassell and Kearney Horse Auction Mart was one option. Formed as a general auction house in the 1870s, the company began specializing in show horses and elegant carriages for the city's elite, operating several equine auction buildings along East 13th Street. *(cited from: https://ephemeralnewyork.wordpress.com/2016/06/30/the-1904-horse-auction-house-in-the-east-village/)*

Some carriage houses incorporated "horse walks" - interior passageways that allowed a horse to walk from the street to a stable. Dense urban areas like New York City still have evidence of these discrete entrances, an unadorned, mysterious entry without a stoop that opens to the sidewalk. The horse walk door is the brown door at this house at 7 Leroy Street in Greenwich Village, a Federal-style beauty built-in 1831. Behind this door is the horse walk, a narrow passageway through which a homeowner's horse was led from the street to a separate carriage house or stable behind the main house. *(cited from: https://ephemeralnewyork.wordpress.com/2012/01/24/the-horse-walks-hiding-in-greenwich-village/)*

Horses must drink, but urban settings rarely have convenient streams with clean water. New York is a city of enchanting water fountains. Some of the most beautiful were intended for horses, thousands of which packed the streets daily for 3 centuries, doing the labor needed to build the city. All these horses needed places to rehydrate, like the Hamilton Fountain at Riverside Drive and 76th Street. Funds to build the fountain were bequeathed to the city by Alexander Hamilton's great-grandson, a wealthy property owner, who died in 1890. *(cited from: https://ephemeralnewyork.wordpress.com/2012/12/08/lovely-fountains-for-city-horses-and-other-animals/)*

Mounting blocks were found on many streets in the cities, like this one in Mobile, Alabama, for people to get on their horses and into carriages.

Hitching posts and tethering rings were also in many places throughout the cities. Some hitching posts were elaborate like this one next to a mounting block in the Garden District in New Orleans.

Tethering rings are discreet metal loops embedded in walls, sidewalks, and curbs. In 1907 Portland City Council passed an ordinance requiring that new curbs in front of houses have "ring bolts" installed every 25 feet. This was so that delivery vehicles could be securely tied down to protect pedestrians and other wagons using the street. *(cited from: https://alamedahistory.org/2018/06/12/portlands-horse-tethering-rings/)*

(Information for Horse Relics Still Found in Cities. (cited from: http://mentalfloss.com/article/83608/10-relics-horse-powered-city)

Tethering ring attached to sidewalk.

Urbanization - The Population Shift to the Cities

In 1775 James Watt patented the steam engine, a machine that would become a symbol of the industrial revolution. After refining the steam engine, James Watt invented a standard measure of mechanical work–33,000 foot-pounds of work per minute, or 1 horsepower. This unit allowed customers to estimate how many horses an engine could replace and to gauge whether replacing their horses would be economical. In many cases, it was not.

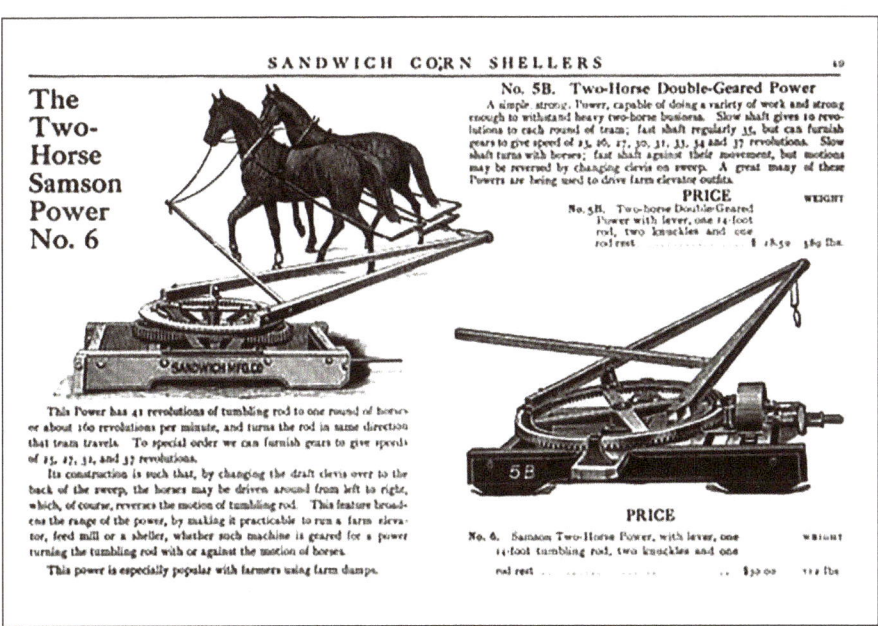

Horses were hooked up to engines through circular sweeps, rotating platforms and treadmills.

For much of the 19th century, horses were the engine of choice for applications that required flexibility or mobility and for businesses that could not afford a large capital outlay. They were hooked up to engines through circular sweeps, rotating platforms, treadmills, and harnessed two vehicles on wheels and tracks.

Horses were the catalysts for the paving of streets and the urbanization of cities. *(cited from: https://theblobologist.wordpress.com/2013/05/12/horsepower/)*

The new technologies of the late 1800s led to a massive leap in industrialization, requiring large numbers of workers. New electric lights and powerful machinery allowed factories to run 24 hours a day, 7 days a week requiring workers to live close to the factories. While the work was dangerous and difficult, many Americans were willing to leave behind the declining prospects of agriculture in the hope of better wages in industrial labor. Problems from famine to religious persecution led to a new wave of immigrants. They arrived from central, eastern, and southern Europe, many found work near the cities where they first arrived.

Rapid urbanization in cities

The most common form of transportation within cities was the horse railway (omnibus/trolley). By 1886 there were 525 horse railways in 300 cities in the U.S.; a generation had adapted to their use, and urban development patterns began to change. Factory workers were no longer forced to accept housing in dark and dingy tenements next to a factory. The workman could commute on a horsecar and railway system. This was a primary driving agent that allowed a dispersion and separation of residential from commercial land uses. Local merchants usually had a significant increase in trade after the start of a new horsecar line on the street in front of their establishments. *(cited from: http://www.foundsf.org/index.php?title=The_Heyday_of_Horsecars and https://courses.lumenlearning.com/ushistory2os2xmaster/chapter/urbanization-and-its-challenges/)*

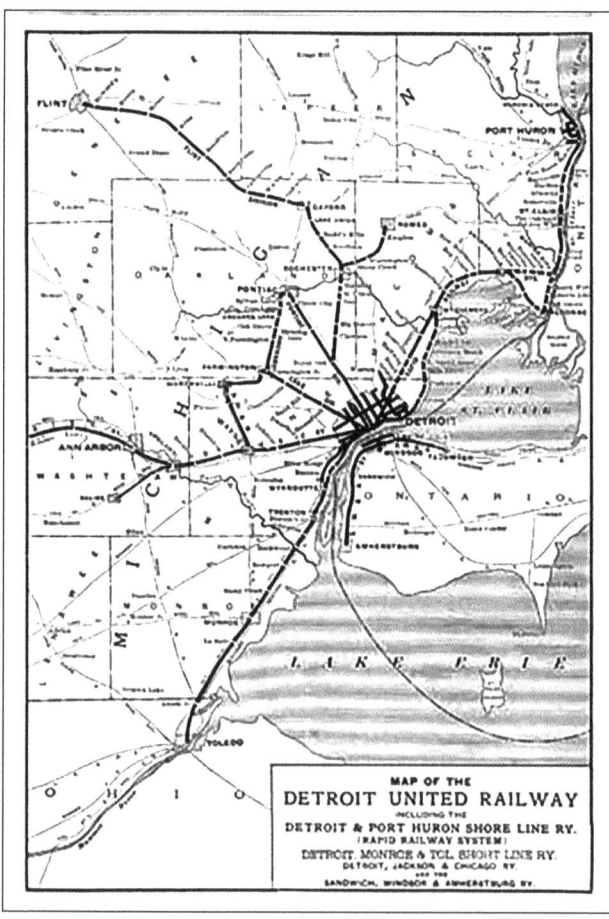
Horsecar and Railway systems in Detroit, 1900

Omnibuses were pulled by horses on rails, and these tracks often transitioned over to be used by electric cars. During the turn of the last century, horses and electric vehicles would sometimes be traveling side-by-side.

San Francisco is well known for its cable cars. Initially, horses pulled the trolleys up and down the hills in San Francisco. Andrew Smith Hallidie tested the first cable car at four o'clock in the morning, August 2, 1873, on San Francisco's Clay Street. His idea for a steam engine-powered, cable-driven rail system was conceived in 1869. He came up with this idea after witnessing horses being whipped while they struggled on the wet cobblestones to pull a horsecar up Jackson Street. *(cited from: https://www.sfmta.com/getting-around/muni/cable-cars/cable-car-history)*

So Many People with So Many Needs

Horses were the central cog in the 19th-century urban economy! Horses were vital when it came to ground transport within the city. City horses hauled everything from steel to home delivery of milk. They powered ferries and pulled trolleys. Goods from the expanded railway and steamboat lines could only be distributed to their final destinations under the power of horses. This forced the horse-drawn transports to grow more efficiently in parallel with steam technology. Innovations in breeding produced larger horses. These more powerful horses could pull larger loads. *(cited from: https://theblobologist.wordpress.com/2013/05/12/horsepower/)*

New York City, 1917

These industrial-strength horses were honored every year in a parade in New York. The first annual Work Horse Parade was held in New York City on Memorial Day 1907. Over 1,000 horses, ranging from beer and ice wagon teams to fire and police horses, paraded through the city. According to a May 19, 1907 article in the New York Daily Tribune, "places of honor will be given to the horses longest in service, best cared for and most considerately handled." Spectators lined the route to see the teams of delivery and draft horses, and medals and prizes were awarded. *(cited from: ttps:// blogs. loc. gov/picturethis/2015/10/work-horses-pulling-their-weight/)*

Work Horse Parade, 5/30/09. Photo by Bain News Service

Before the invention of refrigeration in the early twentieth century, ice was harvested every winter. Large ice plows were pulled by horses to cut deep grooves into the surface of a frozen pond. Usually, one man walked beside the horse to keep it going in a straight line. A second man followed behind the horse and held the handles of the plow. The ice was stored in large ice houses, the proprietors of which sold ice to shippers of fresh fish, waterfowl, and produce for train deliveries to large cities. City dwellers had ice delivered to them by horse and wagon. The iceman had to lift from 25 to 100-pound blocks. Block size was determined by the consumer. Customers would put a numbered card in the window. The number would correspond with the

number of pounds of ice they wanted. The ice was weighed on a spring scale on the truck, but an experienced delivery man could estimate the weight. The ice was carried to a kitchen using ice tongs and chipped with chisels to fit the compartment of the icebox. *(cited from: http://frozen61.tripod.com/id5.html)*

Cities were full of all sorts of delivery trucks going to homes as well as two businesses. The horse and milk wagon were a famous sight. Wayne Creamery kept their horses and milk wagons into the 1960s! The horses knew the route and would walk from house to house without even being driven! People knew the names of their delivery horses, and children would run out to offer the horses sugar cubes and apples.

Mary Chris Foxworthy's grandfather, Henry Johnson, owner of Wayne Creamery in Detroit.

Many types of horse-drawn vehicles kept the city functioning. Fire and Police departments and ambulances–all powered by horses! To learn more about the exciting history of horse-drawn fire engines, be sure to read the Equine Heritage Institute book: The Fire Horse: A Historical Look at Horses and Firefighting.

Mail Delivery

City Bakery Delivery

Oil Delivery

Grocery Delivery

Garbage Removal

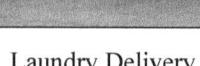

Laundry Delivery

Police Patrol

Firefighting Engine

Waterloo Brewery

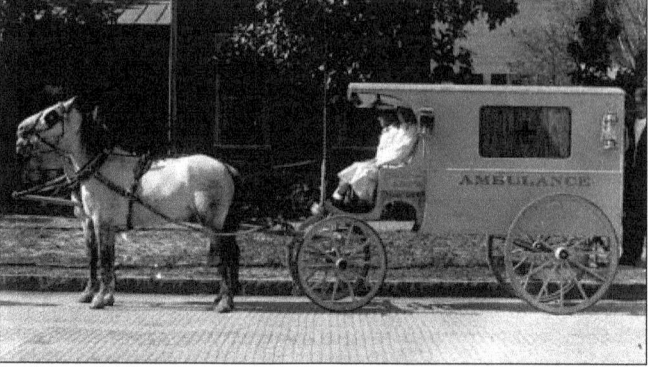

Ambulance

Even though mass transit was provided in many cities, many people preferred a more private means of transportation, such as a hansom cab. Numerous people owned personal means of transportation as well. Like today's countless choices in cars, trucks, and SUVs that serve the needs and tastes of consumers, carriages and buggies were all different to serve the needs and tastes of the owner.

Some vehicles were used explicitly for park driving. Phaetons with a high, sweeping dash became popular for driving in the park by ladies. The Wicker Phaeton (left below) and George IV phaeton (right below) are vehicles that would have been used for Park Driving.

Much like the minivans of today, some carriages were family vehicles. They were used for quick trips to town, running errands, visiting friends, and going to church. Runabouts (left) and Surreys (right) fall into this category.

There were carriages specifically for traveling. The mail phaeton might be used for pleasure driving or for traveling by "post," that is, making a journey by stages, using hired post-horses driven postilion by a postboy. It came to be the ultra-gentleman's driving carriage. The mail phaeton was designed for use with a pair of horses, and two grooms in livery would typically be carried on the rear seat. *(cited from: https://www.carriageassociationofamerica.com/carriage-tour)*

This unusual photo, shows a woman driving a mail phaeton put to a single – proving that even then, people did what suited them!

The Bronson Wagon was a less formal carriage used for traveling.

Some vehicles were used for sporting activities. The Dogcart is a common carriage among collectors. It was made with a ventilated compartment used to carry hounds to the fox hunt. Similarly, the Cocking Cart was used to accommodate fighting cocks. As in the case of the Dogcart, these carriages developed into pleasure carts. They were rarely used to transport either cocks or hounds. *(cited from: https://www.carriageassociationofamerica.com)*

A Dog-Cart was used to carry hounds to the fox hunt.

A Cocking Cart was used to accommodate fighting cocks.

Another method of conveyance for traveling was coaching. The demanding sport of driving a heavy road coach pulled by four horses was an appealing way for the elite to display wealth and impress others during the late 19th and early 20th century. A related vehicle was the Park Drag-similar in look but slightly lighter than the Road Coach. It was extremely popular as an outing vehicle for wealthy gentlemen, their families, and friends. The Park Drag experience was about the fun and also about being seen in places like New York's Central Park in view of admiring spectators. Passengers atop of the coach had a great view of events such as horse races, enjoyed picnics in the country, and partied at homes of the elite in Newport, Rhode Island. Servants sat inside the vehicle, ready to serve food and drinks carried in specially constructed compartments inside and outside the vehicle. Coaching is still popular today! *(cited from: https://www.thehenryford.org/collections-and-research/digital-collections/artifact/27990)*

Gloria Austin and her Healy Park Drag

Carriages often had multiple uses. The Gig was used for park driving and for the gentleman to drive about the city on business. When horse shows became popular about 1890 and classes for high-stepping horses were introduced, it was considered appropriate for a gentleman to drive his high-stepper to a gig.

The Gig

Tandem driving with a Gig or other high two-wheeled vehicle such as a Dog Cart was a popular way to transport a horse to a location; think of it as the horse trailer of today! The lead horse in the tandem did not pull the carriage. Once arriving at the destination, perhaps a fox hunt, the lead horse would be unhitched and ridden while the wheel horse (the horse pulling the carriage) would rest up for the journey home. Tandem driving is very challenging, and it soon became a form of driving in the park for a whip (driver) to show off his/her driving skills. *(cited from: https://www.carriageassociationofamerica.com/carriage-tour/stanhope-gig/)*

Tandem driving with a Gig.
Driver, Ms. Amy Lee Golisano,
granddaugher of Gloria Austin,
accompanied by Coachman David Sanders.

In the 21st century, we worry about the power grid going out and the country coming to a screeching halt. In the 19th century, the dependence on the horse in the cities was as important as our power grids of today. Horses powered the economy.

In 1872 an outbreak of the equine flu, which became known as the Great Epizootic, swept across the nation like wildfire. The epidemic brought the entire U.S. economy to a virtual standstill. Imagine a transportation disaster that within 90 days affected every aspect of American transportation, everything Americans took granted, everything that ensured their safety, every city, town, and village where they lived and left everything in its path under siege. (The Long Riders' Guild Academic Foundation founder CuChullaine O'Reilly) Official estimates put the number of affected horses at between 80% and 99%. Ports and transportation came to a standstill. Firemen were reduced to pulling their own fire equipment. The outbreak forced men to pull wagons by hand, while trains and ships full of cargo sat unloaded, tram cars stood idle, and deliveries of basic community essentials were no longer being made. Locomotives also came to a halt as coal could not be delivered to power them. One of the major casualties of the Great Epizootic was the city of Boston itself. A great fire swept through the industrial section on November 9, ultimately destroying 26 hectares of the city, comprising 776 buildings. (Read more about Fire Horses in the Equine Heritage book, The Fire Horse: A Historic Look at Horses and Firefighting.) The

Cartoon about the Great Epizootic, equine flu.

November 1872 issue of Harper's Weekly. The horse plague - sketches about town during the epidemic by Theo R. Davis.

Great Epizootic was the worst equestrian catastrophe in the history of the United States–and perhaps the world. *(cited from: https://www.horsetalk.co.nz/2014/02/17/how-equine-flu-brought-us-standstill/)*

This drawing, appearing in a November 1872 issue of Harper's Weekly, shows city life under the pall of the Great Epizootic. The "temporary expedients" (see bottom corner) included the use of handcarts and wheelbarrows, men pulling wagons, and the conscription of oxen for the heavier loads. *(cited from: https://www.pantagraph.com/news/local/great-epizootic-of-brought-commerce-to-a-standstill/article_a7f6135b-6803-5018-aeb5-a8003f8b9759.)*

Sometimes we might wish that we could live in a more tranquil and perhaps even romantic era. But having hundreds and thousands of horses in the cities was not as idealistic as it may seem. Health officials in Rochester, New York, calculated in 1900 that the 15,000 horses in that city produced enough manure in a year to make a pile 175 feet high covering an acre of ground and breeding 16 billion flies, each one a potential spreader of germs. *(cited from: "Urban Pollution — Many Long Years Ago," American Heritage, 1971)*

The streets of cities were "literally carpeted with a warm, brown matting . . . smelling to heaven." Crossing Sweepers would offer their services to pedestrians, clearing out paths for walking, but when it rained, the streets turned to muck. When it was dry, the wind whipped up the manure dust and choked the citizenry.

Writing in the Times of London in 1894, one writer estimated that in 50 years every street in London would be buried under 9 feet of manure. Moreover, all these horses had to be stabled, which used up ever-larger areas of increasingly valuable land. As the number of horses grew, ever-more land had to be devoted to producing hay to feed them rather than producing food for people. It seemed that urban civilization was doomed. Of course, urban civilization was not ultimately buried in manure. The great crisis vanished when millions of horses were replaced by motor vehicles. *(cited from: https://fee.org/articles/the-great-horse-manure-crisis-of-1894/)*

World War I

When the war began, the British army had a mere 25,000 horses. That may seem like a lot of horses but, considering that 8 million horses and countless mules and donkeys died in the war, it then seems hard to imagine how the various nations were able to obtain so many horses and mules. Horses were shipped from Spain, Portugal, New Zealand, South Africa, India, Canada, and America.

At one point, America was sending 1,000 horses a day. Beginning in late November 1914, the port of Newport News, Virginia, became the biggest shipper of American war horses and mules to the British army in Europe is a crucial effort that helped the Allies win the war. Killing American horses and mules became a strategic priority for the Germans. A German sabotage campaign was the first attempt at using germs in warfare. Clandestine attempts by German agents to infect and kill the horses were not even discovered until after the war.

A QF 13-pounder of the Royal Horse Artillery moving into position on the Western Front during World War I

At the outbreak of the war, Americans owned between 24 and 25 million horses and 4½ million mules. There were 2 million horses in the United Kingdom, 3.2 million in France, 1 million in Italy, 4.5 million in Germany and 1.8 million in Austria. More than half the horses on earth lived in the United States and Russia. (cited from: from US Department of Agriculture Yearbook 1920 pp. 701-717, table 229) The U. S continued to have a robust horse and mule population throughout the war years due to the Federal Government encouraging peak production of foodstuffs with the "Food Will Win the War" slogan.

Captain Sidney Galtery, an English Remount Officer, had the job of supervising the handling of horses in France from their arrival on ships through the casting of horses. His book, "The Horse and the War," is a detailed accounting of the War Horse in World War I. He commented on the American horses that were shipped to Europe that "… of all the breeds and cross-breeds of horses in the world the one from the United States and Canada has proved paramount and incomparably the best…. Hardiness, the placidity of temper, strength, and power, virility of constitution, with what is called 'good heart,' versatility and extraordinary activity for his size and weight — these are characteristics that have impressed themselves for all time on all who have had to do with him… the light draught of American origin has come to stay in this country. After all, they are a distinct type. Some may be better than others, and some may be heavier in physique than the vast majority, but these latter are as if they had all come out of the same mold. By comparison, the British light draught is a nondescript, a misfit. He could be anything — a half-bred Shire or Clydesdale, a Welsh cob, a heavyish Hackney, a Cleveland bay, or a heavy-weight 'hunter' without true hunter lines and action. All these odds and ends of horse-flesh we have seen pass through remount depots on route to the theatres of war. They were classed as light draught because they were neither heavy draught nor a riding horse. But the Yankee was essentially and absolutely a light draught horse, true to type, varying not at all in character and very little in the non-essential details. He is the real equine hero of the war, and by his triumphs, which must be as real in peacetime as in war, he simply must take his place, and an important one, too, in the horse population of these Islands."

American horses did not come home after the war. There was apprehension in the United States that animals might be returned to the U.S. and carry some disease or infection. W.H. Butler of the Ohio Percheron Breeders' Association wrote a letter to the War Department expressing this concern.

On January 30, 1919, the War Department directed that: "No public animals belonging to the military forces will be imported from Europe to the United States." It was directed, however, that up to 200 private mounts could be imported subject to 90 days in quarantine in Europe, shipment in isolation, and a further 90 days quarantine in the U.S. The officer was also required to verify that he was the owner of the horse. Some U.S. horses that remained were transferred to the Remount Service. Others were sold at 600 public auctions conducted by the A.E.F. in France. The French Government purchased 33,045 animals for distribution to inhabitants of devastated regions. The Polish government bought 5,000, and Belgium bought 400 cavalry horses. Other purchases came from England, Serbia, Switzerland, and Czechoslovakia. The Third Army assigned to Luxembourg and occupation duty in German Rhineland was provided 50,340 animals. In 1921 there was erected in the State, War, and Navy Department Building in Washington, a memorial tablet to commemorate the services of American horses and mules in the war. *(cited from: "Where Have All the Horse Gone," pp 54-58)*

The loss of horsepower in Europe during World War I was devastating. Many European economies could not operate without horses. In the transportation sector, horses still pulled a number of trams, carts in the cities and villages, and even the stagecoaches that were put back into local service in order to overcome the fact that it was impossible for civilians to travel by train. Horses were indispensable for agriculture, both for plowing and for the transportation of foodstuffs. No plant or manufacturing facility could operate without them, both for bringing in the raw materials and for carrying away the finished products. The horses pulled the trucks at the bottom of the mines, brought the ore to the surface and to the loading docks, and pulled the barges on the canals. *(cited from https://www.rtbf.be/ww1/topics/detail_the-horse-an-essential-participant-of-the-great-war?id=8358614)*

Many cities employed circus animals to take the place of the horses. On the farms, plowing was done by hand, and in the cities, carts were pulled by manpower. America's seemingly endless supply of horses and mules were crucial to the Allied victory. While Europe was dealing with the loss of horsepower in the cities and on farms, America had enough horses to supply the war effort AND keep American farms and cities on the move.

To learn more about the horses and mules in World War I, read the Equine Heritage Institute book: The Unsung Heroes of World War I–How Horses, Mules, and Donkeys Changed the First World War.

ON THE MOVE WITHOUT HORSES

North Americans employed 4 million horses in 1840 for agricultural work and travel. By 1900 there were 24 million horses; a six-fold increase in the number of horses! Horses were used to plow fields, as well as pull street trolleys, drays, brewery wagons, city vehicles, omnibuses, and carriages. For every 3 people there trod 1 working horse in the U.S. In comparison, there are now 1.3 people for every car in the U.S.

By 1890 New Yorkers took an average of 297 horse-car rides per person a year. Today, they hail an average of 100 cab rides. In a New York City traffic study undertaken in 1907, horse-drawn vehicles moved at an average speed of 11.5 mph. A similar study conducted almost 60 years later found that automobiles moved through the city's business district at an average speed of only 8.5 mph. *(cited from: https://thetyee. ca/News/2013/03/06/Horse-Dung-Big-Shift/ and https://parkcityhistory.org/wp-content/uploads/2012/04/Teacher-Background-Information.pdf)*

Many of the new technologies developed during World War I eliminated the need for horses. The internal combustion engine took from the horse the distinction it had enjoyed over the centuries as the sole, or primary, source of mobile energy and swept the horses from the road, the farm, and the battlefield. But it took the automobile and tractor nearly 50 years to dislodge the horse from farms, public transport, and wagon delivery systems throughout North America. Not only were horse's jobs gone but gone too were the jobs of all those involved with the horse economy; the teamsters, the hostlers, the grooms, the farriers, wheelwrights, carriage painters, carriage builders, draymen, liverymen, makers of saddle, whips, blankets and other horse clothing, manure transporters–all no longer necessary. Gone too were the jobs of the farmers in the belt of farms around each city, growing the forage to feed the city horses, the hay, and grain dealers. The "job" of the horse became one of companion and teammate in athletic endeavors, hopefully, to never again have to endure the horrors of war on such a large scale. *(cited from: "Where Have All the Horse Gone?", pp 185-86, back cover)*

New York prior to WWI

Horse Breeds of America

Today, there are many breeds of horses in America that are the result of cross-breeding the early breeds as well as crossbreeding many breeds and types of horses.

American Paint Horse - Estimated population over 1,000,000 worldwide

The origins of the Paint Horse in North America can be traced back to the two-toned horses introduced by the Spanish explorers. Inevitably, some of these colorful equines escaped creating the wild herds of horses roaming the Great Plains. Captured and gentled, they raced alongside the vast herds of buffalo and traveled hundreds of miles on cattle drives. Cherished by the finest horsemen of the Western frontier, both Native Americans and cowboys sought the hardy horses loudly splashed with color. Over time, breeders gradually improved the conformation and athletic ability of the rugged descendants of wild mustangs and cow ponies. Each generation passed its unusual and unique coat patterns and coloring to the next, creating the American Paint Horse.

Scout, Tonto's horse on the Lone Ranger

Average Size: 14.2 to 16 hands, Body Type: Western Stock Horse, Colors: Combination of white with common horse colors, Coat Patterns: Tobiano, overo and tovero *(cited from: http://www.ansi.okstate.edu/breeds/horses/paint/index.html/)*

Cochise, Little Joe's horse on Bonanza

THE AMERICAN HORSE - THE IMPORTANCE OF THE HORSE THROUGHOUT AMERICAN HISTORY

American Quarter Horse - Estimated population over 5,000,000 worldwide

The principal development of the Quarter Horse was in the southwestern part of the United States in Texas, Oklahoma, New Mexico, eastern Colorado, and Kansas. Some breed historians have maintained that it is the oldest breed of horses in the United States and that the true beginning of the Quarter Horse was in the Carolinas and Virginia. Nelson, C. Nye, in Outstanding Modern Quarter Horse Sires, has suggested that the Chickasaws secured from the Indians were the true beginning of the Quarter Horse. These were small blocky horses, probably of Spanish extraction, which the planters secured from the Indians, and which were adapted for a variety of uses. The colonists were quite interested in short races, and it was only natural that they should have attempted to increase the speed of their horses; to this end, some of the best early Thoroughbreds brought to the United States were instrumental in the improvement of these local running horses. In 1752, John Randolph of Virginia imported a grandson of The Godolphin Arabian, called Janus. When Janus was bred to Colonial mares bearing the blood of the Chickasaw horse, the result was the prototype of the American Quarter Horse. While it cannot be said that Janus founded the breed, it can be argued convincingly that he shaped and formed it significantly.

Buttermilk - Dale Evans' horse

The early improvement in the Quarter Horse - so-called because of its great speed at one-quarter of a mile - and the early development of the Thoroughbred in the United States was closely associated. Some sires contributed notably to both breeds. Many short-distance horses were registered in the American Stud Book as Thoroughbreds when the Stud Book was established, even though they did not trace in all lines to imported English stock.

It is more logical to assume that the true establishment of the Quarter Horse took place sometime later in the southwest range country rather than in colonial times. It was in the southwest that the true utility value of these short-distance horses was truly appreciated. The cowman found the Quarter Horse quick to start, easy to handle, and of a temperament suitable for handling cattle under a wide variety of conditions. Even in the Southwest, much was unknown of the breeding of many of the horses that were classified and registered in the 1940s as Quarter Horses. It is logical, therefore, to conclude that until the Stud Book was established, and the pedigrees were based on fact rather than on memory and assumptions, the Quarter Horse should have been called a type of horse rather than a breed. It is difficult to give the exact origin of the present-day Quarter Horse. Ranchers tried to breed the kind of horses on which men could work cattle, and that could also be used in the age-old sport of racing. The Quarter Horse was not raced on carefully prepared tracks but was raced on any suitable open space. Organized races were the exception rather than the rule, with many of the races being run as a match race after a private wager between owner or riders. In the Southwest country, as in the East, no particular attention was made to keep short-distance horses as a distinct breed. Fast horses whose offspring made good cow ponies were crossed on the existing stock of mares. Many times, these mares carried Spanish, Arabian, Morgan, or Standardbred breeding. The naming of horses after persons was a common practice, and often when the horses were sold, their names were changed; such practices have led to no end of confusion in attempting to verify pedigrees after the horses, breeders, and owners were deceased. *(cited from: http://www.ansi.okstate.edu/ breeds/horses/quarter/index.html)*

Docs Keepin' Time portrayed Black Beauty in the 1994 film

Modern American Quarter Horses are short and stocky, with heavy muscular development; short, wide heads; and deep, broad chests. They are fast starting, turning, and stopping ability and can maintain speed for short distances. Their colors are variable, but all are solid. The height of mature animals varies from 14.3 to 16 hands, and their weight varies from 950 to 1,200 pounds. They have a calm, cooperative temperament.

George Strait owns Quarter Horses

An American Quarter Horse at work at Barthle Brothers Ranch in Central Florida

American Saddlebred - Estimated population 75,000 worldwide

After the American Revolution, the production of good Saddle Horses became a priority in Kentucky. These animals played a major role in settlement of the upper Ohio Valley. They went south into Tennessee and beyond, and across the Mississippi into Missouri. Animals from Ohio, Indiana, Illinois, Iowa, and Tennessee all made contributions to the breed. Missouri rivaled Kentucky for the best Saddle Horses, and Missourians say, "If Kentucky made the Saddle Horse, then Missouri made him better."

Horse shows became a popular form of public entertainment, often held at fairs. The first recorded show was in Lexington, Kentucky, in 1817, but such competitions undoubtedly took place years before. In 1856, St. Louis, the largest city west of the Mississippi, held its first great fair, which featured the nation's first major horse show.

Denmark, the stallion who would be designated Foundation Sire of the breed, was foaled in 1839. By the time of the Mexican War in 1846, the American Saddlebred was a well-established breed. Entire companies of American volunteers from Kentucky and Missouri, mounted on these horses, fought in Mexico. The American Saddle Horse gained fame as a breed during the Civil War. Since most Confederate horses were privately owned, General Grant's order at Lee's surrender, which allowed the men to keep their horses, perhaps saved the breed. The Confederate commands of Generals John Hunt Morgan and Nathan Bedford Forrest were mounted almost exclusively on American Saddlebreds, and these horses performed legendary feats of endurance during the war.

William Shatner owns and shows Saddlebreds

Traveller owned by Robert E. Lee

After the war, the St. Louis Fair was revived. All breeds had their day in competition at St. Louis, but in the 1870s, the Denmark's became dominant. Because of the increased popularity and commercial value of the Saddlebred, enlightened breeders began to call for the formation of a breed association and registry in the 1880s. Charles F. Mills of Springfield, Illinois, began compiling pedigrees and formulating rules for a registry. The Farmers Home Journal, a newspaper published in Louisville, Kentucky, called for a meeting on April 7, 1891, to organize the association, and the registry was established that day; the first horse breed association in the United States. (cited from: http://www.ansi.okstate.edu/breeds/horses/saddlebred/index.html)

American Saddlebreds come in almost all colors, ranging in height from 14 to 17 hands and weigh 800-1,200 pounds. The head and eye of the ideal American Saddlebred suggest refinement and intelligence. Long, sloping pasterns give a spring to the stride, making American Saddlebreds very comfortable to ride. High quality, smoothness, and balanced proportions complete an overall picture of symmetry and style.

Appaloosa - Estimated population 500,000 worldwide

The Appaloosa's heritage is as colorful and unique as its coat pattern. Usually noticed and recognized because of its spots and splashes of color, the abilities, and beauty of this breed are more than skin deep.

Humans have recognized and appreciated the spotted horse throughout history. Ancient cave drawings as far back as 20,000 years ago in what is now France depict spotted horses as do detailed images in Asian and 17th-century Chinese art.

The Spanish introduced horses to North America as they explored the American continents. Eventually, as these

1936 Kentucky Derby winner Bold Venture

horses found their way into the lives of Indians and were traded to other tribes, their use spread until most of the Native American populations in the Northwest were mounted (about 1710).

The Nez Perce of Washington, Oregon, and Idaho became especially sophisticated horsemen and their mounts, which included many spotted individuals, were prized and envied by other tribes. Historians believe they were the first tribe to breed selectively for specific traits - intelligence and speed - keeping the best and trading away those that were less desirable.

When white settlers came to the Northwest Palouse region, they called the spotted horses "Palouse horses." Over time the name was shortened and slurred to "Appalousey" and finally "Appaloosa."

During the Nez Perce War of the late 1800s, Appaloosa horses helped the Nez Perce avoid battles and elude the U.S. Cavalry for several months. The tribe fled over 1,300 miles of rugged, punishing terrain under the guidance of the famed Chief Joseph. When they were defeated in Montana, their surviving horses were surrendered to soldiers, left behind, or dispersed to settlers. Nothing was done to preserve the Appaloosa until 1938 when a group of dedicated horsemen formed the Appaloosa Horse Club for the preservation and improvement of the diminishing spotted horse. (cited from: http://www.ansi.okstate.edu/breeds/horses/appaloosa/index.html)

Zip Cochise, who was ridden by John Wayne in the 1966 movie "El Dorado"

The base coat color may be any one of many colors and can include dilutes, duns, grays, roans, and other modifying types. Eyes may be any color, including, but not limited to, blue, hazel, green, brown, amber and black. Coat color patterns may vary from a solid pattern, meaning no spotting at all, to multi-spotted to blanket hipped with no spots. Patterns and markings are extremely varied and found in many sizes and combinations with great variations in areas with white backgrounds. Appaloosas can dramatically change its coat pattern throughout its lifetime. No two Appaloosa horses are identically marked.
(from ApHC Standards guide)

Assault (sired by Bold Venture) who won the Triple Crown in 1946

Banker Ponies - Fewer than 200 annual registrations in the United States and estimated global population less than 2,000

The Banker Ponies inhabit the Outer Banks of the Carolinas and are also called Shackleford ponies, Banker Horses, and Ocracoke Ponies. They are believed to be descendants of Spanish horses brought by some first explorers to the area early in the 16th century. The Ocracoke ponies are thought to be descendants of a late 1500s shipwreck, the Tiger which explored the Eastern Seaboard under the direction of Sir Richard Greenville. After landing on Ocracoke, the horses had the island all to themselves for several centuries. The initial bloodlines of these animals were undoubtedly influenced by English horses as well as Spanish during early exploration. However, their blood has remained relatively pure due to their isolation.

Chinky the Banker Pony by Sanford Tousey, Published by Doubleday, Doran & Company, Inc., Garden City, New York, 1937

Features: Average height 13–14.3 hands, the head is simple with a broad forehead and generally convex profile, deep, narrow chest, and short back, often lack chestnuts on hind legs. Traditional Colors: black | chestnut | bay | dun | pinto | buckskin. Temperament: Docile and friendly for feral ponies. Willing to learn and easy to train. *(cited from: http://www.theequinest.com/breeds/banker-pony/)*

Carolina Marsh Tacky - Fewer than 200 annual registrations in the United States and estimated global population less than 2,000

The Carolina Marsh Tacky or Marsh Tacky is a rare breed of horse, native to South Carolina. It is a member of the Colonial Spanish group of horse breeds, which also includes the Florida Cracker Horse and the Banker horse of North Carolina. It is a small horse, well adapted for use in the lowland swamps of its native South Carolina. The Marsh Tacky developed from Spanish horses brought to the South Carolina coast by Spanish explorers, settlers and traders as early as the 16th century. The horses were used by the colonists during the American Revolution, and by South Carolinians for farm work, herding cattle and hunting. There are believed to be only 8 or 9 strains of Spanish colonial horses left in the US, and the Marsh Tacky is now documented as one of them. *(cited from: https://en.wikipedia.org/wiki/Carolina_Marsh_Tacky)*

Once widely used in the Southeast, the Carolina March Tacky was almost extinct by 1950. Marsh Tackies have a unique gait that was recently named the Swamp Fox Trot. Marsh Tackies are level-headed, easy keepers that are excellent for farm work, endurance competitions, trail riding, or hunting.

A pair of marsh tackies take off at the start of their heat during the annual Marsh Tacky Run in March 2012 on Coligny Beach on Hilton Head Island.

The US Coast Guard kept a small band of Banker ponies and Marsh Tackies to patrol the beaches in World War II.

Chickasaw - Extinct

The Indians captured horses from the Spanish who had arrived in the Americas and began to work with them and develop them to meet the needs of Indian life. As the Chickasaw Indians began to breed the little Spanish horses and develop them through haphazard crossbreeding, there began to develop an extremely versatile little horse.

The horse began to play an important part in the life of the Indian. On festive occasions the horses were raced and the man who had the fastest animal was looked upon as a hero. The horses developed by the Chickasaw Indians were the fastest over that distance.

Remington Park in Oklahoma, Enoch Kelly Haney original statue, entitled "Chickasaw Horse and Rider"

Writers of that time referred to the Chickasaw as a breed, and their descriptions give us an excellent picture of the horse. He was small from the standpoint of height, averaging around 13 hands. He was closely coupled and had a very well-developed muscular structure. At short distances he showed great speed but did not have the staying power to run long races.

Nye, in his book, Outstanding Modem Quarter Horse Sires, describes the development of the Chickasaw Horse in the following manner: "In the Carolinas, before the influx of Orientals began to change the whole breeding and racing picture, many of the planters enjoyed match-racing horses at a quarter of a mile. These races, which became quite a popular pastime, were run in the village streets or in any other handy locality where a straightaway of sufficient length could be found. The majority of these colonial sprinting matches were run by Chickasaw Horses, a small blocky type which the planters got from the Indians. These Chickasaws were, in my opinion, the true beginning of the modern Quarter Horse. They were a fixed type to start with, being easily recognized wherever encountered. They were short and chunky, quick to action, but not distance runners. They were the best utility horses of their time."

Of all the Indian horses of the eastern United States, those of the Chickasaw Indian appeared to be the best. At the annual fairs these horses were bought by and traded to the settlers. As late as 1792, the Knoxville Gazette was advertising the services of Piomingo, a celebrated Chickasaw stud, named in honor of a great chief of the Chickasaw tribe.

Other horse breeds eventually became more popular and influential and the Chickasaw was less favored, and the breed began to disappear. Their pedigrees, poorly recorded, were muddled and lost. It wasn't until the mid-1950s that breeders began to take an interest in preservation. This was done by seeking out horses that fit the description and using them to rebuild the line. So, horses that are called Chickasaw horses may look like the type but aren't necessarily descended from the original horses. Some original Chickasaws may exist, however. These can be found in herds on the Outer Banks and the islands of Virginia and the Carolinas, leftovers from a time when the colonists set their livestock free to graze. *(cited from: https://westernhorseman.com/culture/flashbacks/the-chickasaw-horse/ and https://www.ponybox.com/news_details.php?id=3334)*

Choctaw and Cherokee - Fewer than 200 annual registrations in the United States and estimated global population less than 2,000

The Choctaw and Cherokee tribes were avid horse breeders in their original territories within the southeastern United States. The horses they bred were Spanish and were obtained at first from the chain of missions across the deep South and west of the Mississippi in early Spanish colonial days. As the tribes became adept in horse breeding, the quality of the tribal horses gained a good reputation and was specifically mentioned as being excellent in various historic travel journals. Following the government removal in the mid-1800's of the Choctaw and Cherokee tribes from the southeast to what is now Oklahoma, the tribes continued to breed their horses. The basis for the Oklahoma herds was horses brought from the southeast on the "Trail of Tears", but no doubt some western horses were added as well. Since the Choctaw and Cherokee tribes became important as mediators between several of the more western tribes and the US government in the late 1800s, it is likely that exchange of horses between tribes occurred during the many meetings that were held.

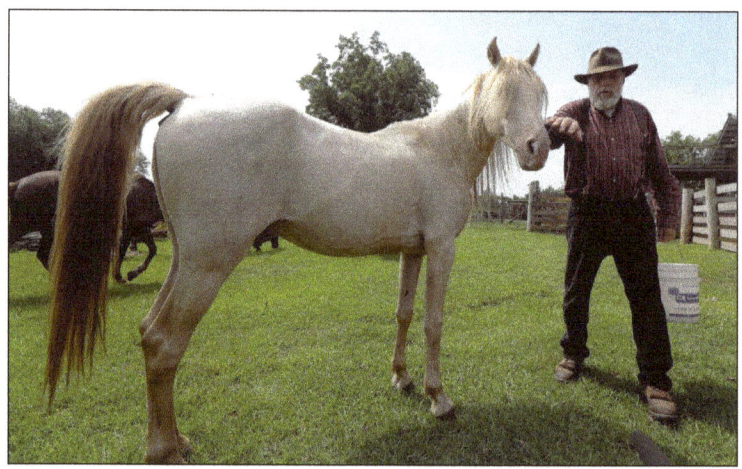

Bill Frank Brown pets DeSoto, a 19-year-old stallion, on his farm in Poplarville, Mississippi. The Texas A&M veterinary school tested samples of the stallions' DNA, and they matched those of Rickman's Choctaws. Gerald Herbert/AP

There were individual families that played an important role in preserving the tribal horses. From the hundreds of Choctaw and Cherokee horses that were available as recently as 1975, The American

Livestock Breed Conservancy estimates that less than 300 pure blooded horses remain as of 2008. This is due to the dispersal of many large herds following the deaths of some of the elderly breeders. Realizing that the once numerous horses were quickly disappearing, Gilbert Jones began the collection of as many pure-blooded horses as he could find and assembled the largest known herd of these animals. Following Gilbert's death in 2001, the horses were inherited by close friends Bryant and Darlene Rickman who remain stewards of the herd and staunch advocates of the Choctaw and Cherokee horse.

Choctaw and Cherokee horses are known for their hardiness, vigor, and adaptability. They are typically easy to train with a gentle hand and can be very people oriented. They make excellent trail and endurance horses but have the potential to do well in any riding discipline. They are all-around easy keepers and according to their owners have little to no health problems. These horses average 14 to 14.2+ hands although some may be larger. Despite their size, they easily carry adults with minimal effort. *(cited from: http://albc-usa.org/ChoctawRescue/crChoctawcherokeehorses.html*

Choctaw mare, right, and her 3-month-old philly colt run with other Choctaw horses on Brown's farm. Gerald Herbert/AP

Chincoteague Ponies - Fewer than 1,000 annual registrations in the United States and estimated global population less than 5,000

Two herds of wild horses make their home on Assateague Island, separated by a fence at the Maryland-Virginia line. These small but sturdy, shaggy horses have adapted to their environment over the years by eating dune and marsh grasses and drinking fresh water from ponds. While they appear tame, they are feral, and Park Rangers urge visitors not to feed or pet them. The Maryland herd is managed by the National Park Service. The Virginia herd is owned by the Chincoteague Volunteer Fire Company. Each year the Chincoteague Volunteer Fire Company purchases a grazing permit from the National Fish and Wildlife Service. This permit allows the Fire Company to maintain a herd of approximately 150 adult ponies on Assateague Island. The Fire Company controls the herd size with a pony auction on the last Thursday in July. Each year tens of thousands of spectators come to watch the Saltwater Cowboys swim the pony herd from Assateague Island to Chincoteague Island. A book was written by Mr. John Amrhein, "The Hidden Galleon," describes the wreck of a Spanish galleon, the La Galga, in 1750. Its location, the circumstances of the voyage, the great storm of 1749, which decimated all the livestock on Assateague Island prior to the La Galga wreck, and the appearance of "Beach" Ponies shortly after the demise of the La Galga, and other evidence strongly suggest this to be the origin of the ponies. While not absolute, the circumstantial evidence he presents is very powerful. For more information, go to www.thehiddengalleon.com. *(cited from: http://www.chincoteague.com/ponies.html)*

In 1947, Marguerite Henry with Misty, published Misty of Chincoteague, the story that made Pony Penning internationally famous. A movie followed, as did several sequel books. The tale of the wild pony Phantom, her foal Misty and the children who buy and raise her have become a classic, still loved and enjoyed by each new generation.

Conestoga Horse - Extinct

The Conestoga Horse (left) was developed in the United States during the 18th and early 19th centuries for pulling the famous Conestoga wagons that were produced in Lancaster County, Pennsylvania. The Conestoga Valley was settled in the early 18th century. It was then wilderness but a country of unsurpassed fertility. Its first homemakers were farmers. They came from the upper Rhine country and Switzerland. With them came a good number of French Huguenots. These people needed horses for many things, all of which were hard work. These horses were not bred by any scientific system but by the process of natural selection. As generation succeeded generation, a horse evolved that met the demands placed upon it by the owner.

It is thought that horses owned by Samuel Gist (who imported the first Thoroughbred to America) and George Washington may have been used for breeding in the development of Conestoga horses.

Benjamin Rush, writing in 1789, states, "A large, strong wagon covered with a linen cloth is an essential part of a German farm. In this wagon, drawn by 4 or 5 horses, a peculiar breed, they convey to market over the roughest roads, 2,000 to 3,000 pounds of produce from their farms." Undoubtedly the horses "of a peculiar breed," which attracted the attention of Dr. Rush, were Conestogas. According to the late Dr. Herbert Beck of Lancaster, who was an authority on horses, the first authentic record which he found on Conestoga horses under that name, appears in "The Cabinet of Natural History and American Rural Sports," published in 1832. Under the heading "The American Horse," 3 breeds are listed. These are the Canadian, the English, and the Conestoga. Of the latter, the writer states, "The Conestoga horse is found in Pennsylvania, long in limb and light in the carcass, sometimes rising to 17 hands." Dr. Beck maintained that it was the only kind of horse bred for that purpose in the United States. As settlers began heading west from Pennsylvania, more and more horses were needed to pull their heavy wagons. The Conestoga wagon was designed to meet this need, and the Conestoga horse was called upon to power it. In hauling these wagons over the Allegheny Mountains, the Conestoga won its place in the story of American transportation. *(cited from: http://articles.mcall.com/1988-03-06/entertainment/2614046_1_five-horsesconestoga-breed)*

It is thought that horses owned by Samuel Gist (who imported the first Thoroughbred to America) and George Washington may have been used for breeding in the development of Conestoga horses.

Florida Cracker Horse - Fewer than 200 annual registrations in the United States and estimated global population less than 2,000

The genetics of the Florida Cracker breed comes from the Iberian horse of the early 16th century Spain and includes blood from the North African Barb, Spanish Sorraia, and the Spanish Jennet. These horses also contributed to the Spanish Mustang, Paso Fino, Peruvian Paso, and Criolla breeds, so the Florida Cracker's genetic base is very similar to theirs.

These horses were used by Florida cowmen, termed "Crackers" from the sound of cow whips cracking, and the name stuck to the horses as well. However, in the 1930s, the Great Depression affected the Florida Cracker breed as severely as it affected most things. Many cattle needed to be transported into Florida to escape the Dust Bowl, but they brought with them the screwworm fly. This new parasite created new challenges in cattle management, and the cattle now required new fencing and dipping vats. The Florida Cracker horse was too small and too weak to meet the cowman's new needs so, they turned to the Quarter Horse to rope and hold cattle for the screwworm treatment. Demand for the Florida Cracker Horse fell, and they became a rarity.

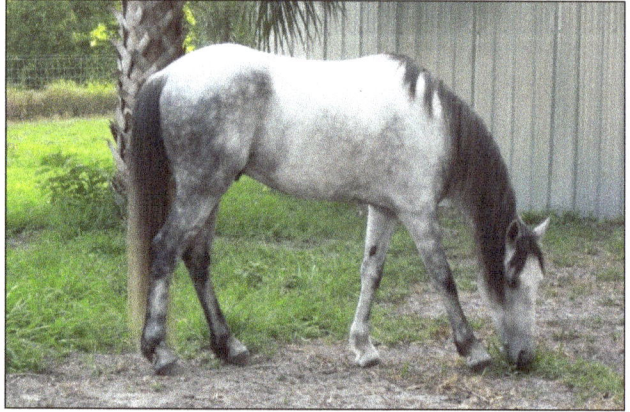

A few families continued the breed, raising them for their own ranches and kept the breed from extinction. In 1989, the Florida Cracker Horse Association was formed to search for the remaining Florida Cracker horses. In May 2008, Florida lawmakers voted the Florida Cracker Horse Florida's official horse.

These horses are small, saddle suited, at 13.2 to 15.2 hands and weigh 700-1000 lbs. They can be any color, although solid colors, namely gray, are most prevalent. Their gaits cover ground well, including the flat-footed walk, running walk, trot, and ambling gait; these are possible with no special shoeing and often even barefooted. They do not share the crested appearance of the neck associated with some Spanish breeds, instead of being fairly narrow and having the same length as the withers-to-croup distance. *(cited from: http://afs.okstate.edu/breeds/horses/florida-cracker-horse)*

Missouri Fox Trotter - Estimated 42,283 registered

Missouri achieved statehood in 1821. The pioneers who poured across the Mississippi River and settled in the Ozarks came largely from Tennessee, Kentucky, and Virginia. Naturally, they brought along their saddle horses, descendants of the early colonial ambling horses, popular in those areas. It soon became apparent that horses able to perform the easy, broken gait called the Fox Trot were the most useful in the rocky, forest-covered hills of the Ozarks, and selective breeding for the Fox Trot gait began. Easy gaited stock imported to our nation's shores during the Colonial era left their genetic imprint on the Fox Trotting Horses of the Ozarks, the American Saddle Horses of Kentucky, and the Walking Horses of Tennessee.

The distinguished characteristic of the Missouri Fox Trotting Horse is the Fox Trot gait; the horse walks with the front feet and trots with the hind feet. This extremely sure-footed gait gives the rider little jar since the hind feet slide into place. The Fox Trot is a rhythmical gait, and the horse can maintain it for long periods of time with little fatigue. The Missouri Fox Trotter also performs a rapid flat foot walk and a delightful canter.

Fox Trotters became the using horse of the Ozarks. They were the favorite mounts of cattlemen, country doctors, sheriffs, and tax assessors before improved roads and cars appeared on the scene. Missouri ranks number two in the nation in cow-calf operations, and Missouri Fox Trotting Horses are historically tied to the grazing cattle industry of the Ozarks. When automobiles made horses almost obsolete in the everyday lives of most Ozarkians, Missouri Fox Trotting Horses survived largely because the cattlemen of the region continued to use and breed them.

Stamina, soundness, and gentle disposition were serious considerations in the breeding of Fox Trotting Horses by pioneer families in the Ozarks. They range from 14 to 16 hands, colors are Black, roan, champagne, brown, cremello, grullo, dun, palomino, buckskin, perlino, coupled with white markings on the face and leg They have a straight face profile, muscular body, medium-length neck ending in withers, well-shaped pointed ears, bright eyes, tapered muzzle, sloped shoulders, short back and sturdy legs, well-proportioned and properly shaped hooves. Missouri Fox Trotters are docile, calm, reliable, placid, goodnatured disposition, loves human company. Missouri Fox Trotters are popular horses for forest rangers due to their comfort, secure footing and reliability on the trails *(cited from: http://afs.okstate.edu/breeds/horses/missourifoxtrotting/index.html)*

Morgan - Estimated 80,000 registered

The Morgan Horse is an America Legend. The breed was the official horse of the American Bicentennial.

The horse known as Justin Morgan's horse started life as a small, rough-coated colt known as "Figure." He was born in 1789, and in 1791, he left his birthplace in Springfield, Massachusetts, with his new owner, the soft-spoken schoolteacher Justin Morgan, by whose name the stallion eventually became known. Although his breeding was unknown (thought to be of Dutch, Thoroughbred, or Arabian breeding), the quality of Justin Morgan's ancestry showed in his straight clean legs; deep muscling over his quarters and shoulders; and fine, intelligent head with large expressive eyes and short, pricked ears. Add to these the quality of his movement, a thick but silky mane and tail, and a clean-cut throatlatch, and you have the conformation of the ideal light horse. Despite these fine qualities, Justin Morgan's lack of size was such that his debt-ridden owner found no buyers on their journey north to Randolph Center, Vermont. It was simply fated that no one but his new owner realized what a little giant he was.

Over the next 30 years, the little bay stallion worked long, hard hours in the fields and on the roads of Vermont. Gradually, the local population began to talk about the feats of "the Justin Morgan horse." Standing just over 14 hands tall, Justin Morgan's exploits gained him fame because he was not as big as colonial workhorses nor as tall and long-legged as racehorses, yet he consistently outperformed both. There was the time he pulled a log no draft horse could budge, the day he had the beauty and spirit to carry President James Monroe on a muster-day parade ground; and the time he outran the most winning racehorse central Vermont had ever known, at least until that day.

Doing it all and doing it well, Justin Morgan remained sound of eye, wind, and limb throughout a lifetime of two ordinary horses. That should have been enough, but the stallion added still more: showy, ground-covering gaits with speed to spare at any one of them; a gentle disposition that made him safe enough for a child to handle yet spirited enough for any horseman, beauty men would recall decades after his death; and rare courage that made men who lost bets on him hit their flagons of rum and say, 'To the little Morgan!' and drink deeply.

Justin Morgan also proved to be one of the greatest breeding horses of all time. As the saga of the little stallion grew, countless mares were bred to him. So prepotent were the genes of this stallion that no matter what type of mare he was bred to, be the mare of the heavy draft or refined racing-type, his offspring inherited his image and abilities. While most breeds develop by breeding horses of similar characteristics to each other, Justin Morgan's ability to pass his characteristics to his offspring for generations to come allowed this single stallion to found an entire breed in his likeness. Today, every registered Morgan traces back to Justin Morgan through his best-known sons Bulrush, Sherman, and Woodbury.

In the coming years, the offspring of these strong, willing, able light horses grew along with the young nation that was building itself upon hard work and determination. In the hands of American colonists, Morgans cleared rugged Vermont mountainsides and converted them into rich farmland. But they weren't mere workhorses, Morgans had the style and elegance to capture the admiration of any city horseman. While some Morgans earned their keep on the farm, others were in high demand to become smart roadsters for Boston and New York financiers. When harness racing reached its heyday in the 1800s, the World's Fastest Trotting Stallion was Ethan Allen 50, old Justin's handsome great-grandson.

As America grew, so did the feats of the Morgan. New England men answered the call of gold and headed for California on Morgans. In the Civil War, the famed Vermont Cavalry was mounted on Morgan horses. The Union's General Sheridan rode his Morgan Rienzi.

In the Indian Wars, the only survivor in the Battle of the Little Big Horn was Keogh's Morgan-bred horse Comanche. If the pathways of history are paved with the bones of the horse, surely America's are paved by Morgans. While the offspring of Justin Morgan was taming the wilderness and building the country, they were also creating the standards by which other American breeds would become known. The stamina and vigor of the Morgan together with his excellent conformation and way of going helped make other American light horse breeds what they are today. The great speed of today's racing Standardbreds was produced by crosses to the fastest Morgan blood. In the 1860s, the Morgan stallion Shepherd F. Knapp was exported to England, where his trotting speed became a byword. Today, many English Hackneys carry his name in their pedigrees.

In American Saddlebreds, such famous champions as Edna May, Bourbon King, Rex Peavine, and Wing Commander trace to Justin Morgan. The foundation sire of the Tennessee Walking horse, Allen F-1, was a grandson of the Morgan stallion Bradford's Telegraph. In addition, many good Morgan mares were sent to Texas only to lose their breed identity in Quarter Horse bands, and to make the breed greater for it. The oldest of all American breeds, the Morgan was strong enough to contribute greatly to almost every other American light horse breed while retaining its own identity across two centuries.

UVM Flash in front of the statue of Justin Morgan (Figure) in Vermont, believed to be in the 1970s, to show conformation consistencies with the original Morgan.

Present-day Morgans differ little from their mighty progenitor. (left: UVM Flash in front of the statue of Justin Morgan (Figure) in Vermont, believed to be in the 1970s, to show conformation consistencies with the original Morgan) The average size of a Morgan today is between 14.2-15.2 hands, with some individuals over or under. Morgan coats are predominantly chestnut, bay, or brown, although many black, palomino, buckskin, and even a few grays appear in the breed. The breed's tremendous courage, disposition, substance, and type has remained as important to breeders today as it was 200 years ago. Whether you visit farms in New England, California, or any state in between, you can see bands of Morgans with the same deep bodies, lovely heads, and straight clean-boned legs. In barns and show rings across the country, the Morgan show horses flash by with heads high, eyes bright, and nostrils wide - Morgan quality showing in every hair on their gleaming, muscular bodies.

Today, Morgans have few wildernesses to conquer or wars to win, but they still accomplish great deeds. They are loved and revered as dynamite performers in Morgan shows across the country, and as loyal, sensible mounts on America's beautiful trails and pathways; they are treasured by mounted police squads and therapeutic riding programs for their intelligence, soundness, and gentleness; they are winning awards in driving, dressage, reining and cutting competitions against horses bred specifically for these jobs; and no matter what they may be doing or the tack they wear, knowledgeable horsemen see them and know, 'That's a Morgan!

Marguerite Henry's popular book, "Justin Morgan Had a Horse," was also made into a movie by Disney.

A bit of the hard-working, determined Morgan legend is with us whenever a Morgan carries a saddle-weary cowhand down a Montana mountain, pulls a carriage around a grueling obstacle course in record time, quietly carries children along a wooded path, or flashes around show rings with a style that causes spectators to cheer. The Morgan, our country's first breed of light horse, is as much a part of America today as it was two centuries ago.'

The Morgan legend has also spread around the world. Morgan owners and clubs can be found in Canada, England, Germany, Italy, France, Australia, New Zealand, Mexico, and South America. The beauty, intelligence, and willing personality of the Morgan will win you over too! (cited from: http://afs.okstate.edu/breeds/horses/morgan/index.html)

Sheffield's Pride (Mansfield x Berry's Bess). Foaled 1942. Bred by RL Berry. Morgan Horse Museum.

Well Known Morgan Horses and Owners

- Many famous officers rode Morgans during the Civil War, and the following regiments of the cavalry were mounted on Morgans at the beginning of the war: First Maine Cavalry, Michigan Cavalry, Third Michigan Cavalry, Fourteenth Pennsylvania Cavalry, Fifth New York Cavalry Company H.

Ruth Worthington and her horse on their ride across Vermont from the collection at the Morgan Horse Museum.

Mustang - Approximately 67,000 roaming on public lands in 10 Western states

The Mustang is a free-roaming horse of the American West. The name was derived from the Spanish word mustengo, which means "ownerless beast" or "stray horse." The original Mustangs were Colonial Spanish horses, but many other breeds and types of horses contributed to the modern Mustang, resulting in varying phenotypes. Since Mustangs are descendants of escaped domesticated horses, wildlife management agencies consider them to be "feral" rather than "wild," although this designation is controversial among mustang advocates. The Bureau of Land Management (BLM) is tasked to uphold the 1971 legislation "The Wild Free-Roaming Horses and Burros Act," written to protect these free-roaming horses. The issue is complex and has many conflicting interests, from those who want to see the horses stay free, to those who object to the strategies used for limiting herd growth, to ranchers who graze their livestock on public land and view the Mustangs as competition. These horses and burros can be found mainly on government-designated Herd Management Areas (HMA) in 10 western states: Arizona, California, Colorado, Idaho, Montana, Nevada, New Mexico, Oregon, Utah, and Wyoming. The Mustang is not on any endangered list at this time, though there are people petitioning to change that. About 100 years ago, about 2,000,000 mustangs roamed the North American terrain, and now there are approximately 67,000. Mustangs are a medium-sized breed of horse. They measure around 14 to 15 hands. Mustangs have a wide variety of colors. They can also have a variety of patches, spots, and stripes. They are a hardy horse, often living to 40 years old. *(cited from: https://www.mnn.com/earthmatters/animals/stories/mustangs-of-the-west-why-this-american-icon-is-disappearing and https://www.livescience.com/27686-mustangs.html)*

- Mustangs average about 56 inches at the shoulder
- They weigh between 700 and 900 pounds
- There are approximately 50,000 mustangs
- Mustangs can run up to 35 miles an hour
- They have one of the longest life spans of horse breeds - sometimes 40 years!

Narragansett Pacer - Extinct

The Narragansett Pacer made valuable contributions to many breeds of North America. The horse is named for the area from which they developed–the Narragansett Bay area of Rhode Island. Their ancestors were probably among the English and Dutch horses, which arrived in Massachusetts between 1629 and 1635. The Dutch horses were 14 hands or over, and the English horses were nearer to 13 hands; most likely Irish Hobby horses. The Narragansett Pacer was known as a saddle horse that provided a comfortable ambling gait that was surefooted; they had great endurance.

Most races in the early colonies were with gaited horses. The Narragansett Pacer was swift indeed! He could pace a mile in just over 2 minutes. Not only were they great horses for

Etching from Frank Forester's Horse and Horsemanship of the United States and British Provinces of North America 1857

racing - a pastime that was very popular–but they also made great saddle horses. Transportation at the time was on rough roads, and the easy ambling gait of the Narragansett Pacer made them incredibly desirable. The Narragansett Pacer was the primary export and chief source of income for the area. It was bred in vast numbers in the 1700s and exported to plantations in Cuba and the Islands. The breed reigned as the most desirable saddle horse for a century and a half.

The breed eventually became extinct as colonial roads improved, and people began to drive trotting horses more than ride these ambling, smooth gaited horses.

The horses were diminutive; 13–14 hands. Despite efforts to increase their size, this never happened due to the system prevalent everywhere of horses roaming at large. The best description of these unusual pacing horses is given by Robert Livingston in an article on American agriculture in the first American edition of the Edinburgh Encyclopedia written about 1830. The description reads as follows:

"They have handsome foreheads, the head clean, the neck long, the arms and legs thin and taper; the hindquarters are narrow and the hocks a little crooked, which is here called sickle hocked, which turns the hind feet out a little: their color is generally, though not always, bright sorrel; they are very spirited and carry both head and tail high. But what is most remarkable is that they amble with more speed than most horses trot so that it is difficult to put some of them upon a gallop. Notwithstanding this facility of ambling, where the ground requires it, as when the roads are rough and stony, they have a fine, easy single-footed trot. These circumstances, together with their being very sure-footed, render them the finest saddle horses in the world; they neither fatigue themselves nor their rider. It is generally to be lamented that this invaluable breed of horses is now almost lost by being mixed with those imported from England and from other parts of the United States." The sturdy qualities of the Narragansett pacers have also been perpetrated by  James Fenimore Cooper in his tales of the American wilderness. He seats his heroine, Alice Munro, on a Narragansett Pacer in The Last of the Mohicans. The horses were evidently still obtainable in Cooper's day, and he must have been an admirer of the breed, for he brings them into his stories frequently. *(cited from: https://archive.org/stream/horseraisinginco00phil/horseraisinginco00phil_djvu.txt)* The British politician Edmund Burke wrote an Account of the European Settlements in America in 1857 that noted the emerging breeds of horses in New England: "They have, besides, a breed of small horses which are extremely hardy. They pace naturally though in no very graceful or easy manner; but with such swiftness, and for so long a continuance, as must appear almost incredible to those who have not experienced it." *(cited from: http://www.newenglandhistoricalsociety.com/narragansett-pacer-lost-horse-new-england-colonies/)*

Well Known Narragansett Pacers and Owners

- George Washington owned a pair of Narragansett Pacers, which he highly valued. He wrote about racing them in his diary.
- Esther Forbes, Paul Revere's Pulitzer Prize-winning biographer, argues forcibly that the horse that Revere rode from Charlestown to Lexington was a Narragansett Pacer, but this has been debated.

Rocky Mountain Horse - Estimated 14,500 registered

Tradition has it that around the turn of the century, a young horse appeared in eastern Kentucky that gave rise to a line of horses that have been prized and treasured in this part of the country ever since. The basic characteristics are of a medium-sized horse of gentle temperament with an easy ambling four-beat gait. This gait made it the horse of choice on the farms and the rugged foothills of the Appalachians. It was a horse for all seasons. It could pull the plows in the small fields, work cattle, be ridden bareback by 4 children to the fishing hole, or to town comfortably on Saturday. They even performed well hitched to the buggy. Fancy barns and stalls were not necessary. Because of its cold-blooded nature, it tolerated the winters in Kentucky with a minimum of shelter. For these reasons, in small groups, the breed was preserved, sustained, and gradually increased in the area. Naturally, outcrossing with the local horses did occur, but the basic characteristics of a strong genetic line have continued.

In Spout Springs, Kentucky, on the farm of Sam Tuttle, these horses found a nurturing ground. Sam, who had the concession for horseback riding at the Natural Bridge State Park, used these horses for many years to haul green and inexperienced people over rough and rugged trails. Old Tobe, his most treasured stallion, who fathered fine horses up until the ripe old age of 37, was as "sure footed" and as gentle a horse as could be found. He was the one that carried the young, the old, or the unsure over the mountain trails of Kentucky, without faltering, even though a breeding stallion. Everyone who rode the stallion fell in love with him. He had the perfect gait and temperament. Many of the present Rocky Mountain Horses carry his bloodline.

The breed is known for gentleness. It is an easy keeper and a wonderful riding horse with a strong heart and endurance. Today the Rocky Mountain Horse is being used as a pleasure horse, for the trail, and competitive or endurance riding. As show horses, the breed is rapidly gaining in popularity because of its beauty and unique way of moving in the ring. The calm temperament of this horse makes it ideally suited for working around cattle and for 4-H projects. These horses have a lot of natural endurance, they are sure-footed on rough ground and, because of their gait, they require a minimum of effort by both horse and rider so that together they can cover a greater distance with less tiring.

It is obvious that the haphazard and unorganized maintenance of this breed would eventually result in dissipation and loss. For this reason, in the summer of 1986, those who were interested in the breed got together to form the Rocky Mountain Horse Association. The purpose of this association is to maintain the breed to increase the number of horses in the breed and expand knowledge of this fine horse. To that end, the association has established a registry that has shown steady and well-regulated growth in the number of horses registered. It is critical that standards be maintained and a panel of examiners has been set up by the association to provide vigorous supervision to the growth and development of the breed. To achieve this, ALL horses must be examined for breed characteristics and approved prior to breeding. The established characteristics for the breed are: (1) The horse must be of medium height from 14.2 to 16 hands, a wide chest sloping 45 degrees on the shoulder with bold eyes and well-shaped ears. (2) The horse must have a natural ambling four-beat gait (single foot or rack), with no evidence of pacing. When the horse moves, you can count four distinct hoofbeats, which produce a cadence of equal rhythm just like a walk, left hind, left fore, right hind, right fore. Each individual horse has its own speed and natural way of going, traveling at 7-20 miles per hour. This is a naturally occurring gait present from birth that does not require training aids or action devices. (3) It must be of good temperament and easy to manage. (4) All Rocky Mountain Horses have a solid body color. Facial markings are acceptable so long as they are not excessive. There may not be any white above the knee or hock. *(cited from: http://afs.okstate.edu/breeds/horses/rockymountain/index.html)*

Standardbred

The origin of the Standardbred traces back to Messenger, an English Thoroughbred foaled in 1780 and exported to the United States in 1788. He was used to improving running horses in America, but when a reform movement began putting pressure on the breeders of runners, trotting horse owners started breeding Messenger with their mares. For unknown reasons, Messenger never raced, but his offspring became the fastest and best-gaited trotters.

Rysdyk's Hambletonian by Currier and Ives

Messenger was the great-grandsire of Hambletonian (left: Rysdyk's Hambletonian by Currier and Ives), a famous trotter that became the foundation of the Standardbred breed. He was foaled in 1849 in New York. His dam was called the Charles Kent mare and was sired by a horse named Abdalla. Hambletonian was owned by a hired hand, William Ryskyk. His offspring dominated trotting races of the day. Messenger and Hambletonian were bred to Narraganset Pacers, Morgans, and Thoroughbreds

The name "Standardbred" was first used in 1879, because, in order to be registered, every Standardbred had to be able to trot a mile within the "standard" of 2 minutes and 30 seconds. Today, many Standardbreds race much faster than this original standard, with several pacing the mile within 1 minute, 50 seconds, and trotters only a few seconds slower than pacers. Slightly different bloodlines are found in trotters than pacers though both can trace their heritage back to Hambletonian. The studbook was formed in 1939, with the formation of the United States Trotting Horse Association.

The first trotter to go less than 2:00 (Readville, Massachusetts, 1903), Lou Dillon, by Sidney Dillon-Lou Milton,

Lou Dillon was the first Standardbred to trot the mile in less than 2 minutes. This talented, but temperamental mare performed this feat in Memphis, Tennessee, but was a west-coast horse, foaled in 1898 near Santa Ynez, California. High strung and hard to handle, she would only stay on her food when mixed with mashed carrots. She traveled extensively to as far away as Berlin, Moscow, and Vienna to entertain spectators with her extraordinary abilities.

Dan Patch was the first Standardbred to pace the mile in less than 2 minutes. The race in Lexington, Kentucky, was official (1:55 ¼ in 1905). The faster time of 1:55 was entered at the Minnesota State Fair in 1906 but was considered unofficial. This famous horse was foaled in Oxford, Indiana, in 1896 and broke the speed record 14 times in the early 1900s. Dan Patch lost only two heats and never lost a race in his career. His record for the fastest pacing race stood for 54 years.

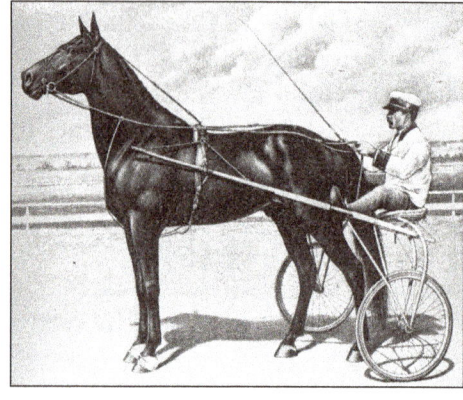

Dan Patch (1896 – 1916) was a noted American Standardbred pacer.

Standardbreds are able to perform the pace and all other horse gaits, including the canter. Standardbreds are best known for their level and sensible dispositions and are generally considered "easy keepers." Standardbred horses have refined, solid legs and powerful shoulders and hindquarters. Standardbreds have a wide range of height, from 14.1 to 17+ hands and most often are bay or the darker variation of bay called "brown," although other colors are not uncommon. Standardbreds are incredibly versatile. You will see them in dressage, jumping, eventing, western, endurance, parades, police work, search and rescue.

Don Dorado wins the 2013 Pennsylvania Sire Stakes, Trainer Bob Baggit, Jr., Driver Tim Tetrick, and Owner Kelly Walker.

Tennessee Walker

The Civil War provided the opportunity for crossbreeding of the Confederate pacers with Union trotters, thus creating the Plantation Walking Horse. The horse gained popularity for the ease of its gaits and ability to stride with ease over hills and valleys in the rocky middle Tennessee terrain. Infused with the blood of Morgans, Standardbreds, and Thoroughbreds, the Tennessee Walker came into being. The breed is seen in a variety of colors, including brown, black, bay, chestnut, roan, palomino, white or gray. Their face, legs, and body may also be marked with white. Tennessee walkers are 14.3 to 17 hands and weigh about 900 to 1,200 pounds. They have a long graceful neck, short back, well-built hindquarters, sloping shoulders, slender but strong legs, and sound feet. The Tennessee Walker's head is handsome and refined with bright eyes, prominent nostrils, and pointed well-shaped ears. Their manes and tails are usually left long and flowing.

Trigger Jr. (Allen's Gold Zephyr), owned by Roy Rogers, was a Tennessee Walking Horse. This breed is particularly appreciated for its three smooth gaits.

The Tennessee Walking Horse became an officially recognized breed in 1950.

Showcasing the Natural Gait of the walking horse in the Pleasure Division.

Thoroughbred - Estimated 1.3 million in the United States

Although the Thoroughbred is not a uniquely America breed, the early Thoroughbreds in America greatly influenced many of our American breeds. There are records of horse racing on Long Island as far back as 1665. The introduction of organized Thoroughbred racing to North America is traditionally credited to Governor Samuel Ogle of Maryland, through whose instigation racing "between pedigreed horses, in the English style" was first staged at Annapolis in 1745. As the country developed, so did Thoroughbred racing, spreading across the nation from coast to coast until today the volume of racing in America far outweighs that of any other country in the world. American bloodlines, too, have come to be respected in the four corners of the earth. In the early days, Thoroughbred breeding records were sparse and frequently incomplete, it is the custom, among other things, not to name a horse until it had proved outstanding ability. It was left to James Weatherby, through his own research and by the consolidation of a number of privately kept pedigree records, to publish the first volume of the General Stud Book. He did this in 1791, listing the pedigrees of 387 mares, each of which could be traced back to Eclipse, a direct descendant of the Darley Arabian; Matchem, a grandson of the Godolphin Arabian; and Herod, whose great-great grandsire was the Byerly Turk. The General Stud Book is still published in England by Weatherby and Sons, Secretaries to the English Jockey Club.

Exercising a Thoroughbred

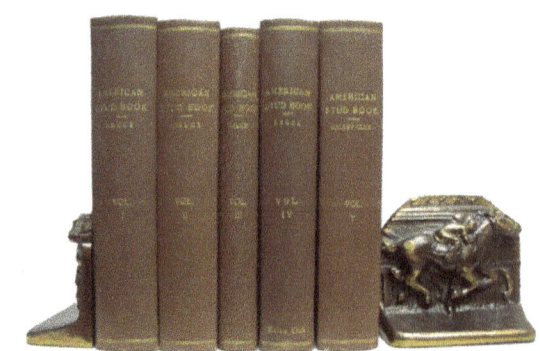

American Stud Book Vol I, Vol II, Vol III, Vol IV, Vol V. Col. Sanders D. Bruce

Several years later, as racing proliferated in the fast-expanding continent of North America, the need for a pedigree registry of American-bred Thoroughbreds, similar to the General Stud Book, became apparent. The first volume of The American Stud Book was published in 1873 by Col. Sanders D. Bruce, a Kentuckian who had spent almost a lifetime researching the pedigrees of American Thoroughbreds. Bruce closely followed the pattern of the first General Stud Book, producing 6 volumes of the register until 1896, when the project was taken over by The Jockey Club. The integrity of The American Stud Book is the foundation on which all Thoroughbred racing in North America depends. The Jockey Club manages one of the most sophisticated computer operations in the country. Its database holds the names of more than 1,800,000 horses on a master pedigree file, names which trace back to the late 1800s. The system also handles daily results of every Thoroughbred race in North America, as well as processing electronically transmitted pedigree and racing data from England, Ireland, France, and other leading Thoroughbred racing countries around the world. What began as a pastime and sporting amusement for the wealthy has now become a worldwide multi-million-dollar industry whose economic impact is widely felt at regional and national levels. From license fees and direct taxes on pari-mutuel, Thoroughbred racing generates nearly $500,000,000 in government revenue each year. But this is relatively minor in comparison to the overall urban and rural economic contribution made by the wide and varied infrastructure of the racing and breeding industry as a whole. A recent estimate, for example, but the industry's contribution to the economy of New York State alone at more than $1.8 billion each year.

The average height of today's Thoroughbred is a little over 16 hands, as opposed to the 14-hand average height of the horses from which the breed originated. The best guidelines for good conformation come from an appreciation of what the body is required to do. Four slender legs must carry more than 1,000 pounds of body weight over extended distances, traveling at speeds of 35-40 miles per hour, yet still, have the strength and suppleness to respond to changes of pace or direction as dictated by racing conditions. Although mechanical and engineering formulas can be used to measure the most desirable dimensions and angles of the body's components, there is no way to measure the most important qualities of Thoroughbred -- its courage, determination, and will. *(cited from: http://afs.okstate.edu/breeds/horses/thoroughbred/index.html)*

Secretariat 1973 Triple Crown winner

David Racing LLC

The Horse in America Today

According to the American Horse Council 2017 Economic Impact Study, the equine industry in the U.S. generates approximately $122 billion in total economic impact, an increase from $102 billion in the 2005 Economic Impact Study. The industry also provides a total employment impact of 1.74 million and generates $79 billion in total salaries, wages, and benefits. The current number of horses in the United States stands at 7.2 million. Texas, California, and Florida continue to be the top 3 states with the highest population of horses. 38 million, or 30.5%, of U.S. households, contain a horse enthusiast, and 38% of participants are under the age of 18. Additionally, approximately 80 million acres of land is reserved for horse-related activities. *(cited from: http://www.horsecouncil.org/press-release/ahcf-announces-results-2017-economic-impact-study/)*

Roy Rogers and Trigger

If the horses are not being used for farming or transportation or industry– WHAT ARE ALL OF THESE HORSES DOING?!

It didn't take long for people to miss the horses - movies and television romanticized horses and created plenty of horse "stars."

Alan Young (Wilbur Post) and Bamboo Harvester (Mr. Ed)

The Lone Ranger and Silver

Hop Along Cassidy and Topper

Gene Autry and Champion

Joey and Fury

The horses of Bonanza

Tex Ritter and White Flash

Horse crazed children imagined themselves owning a horse and saving the day or riding into the sunset and soon many horse toys and products flooded the market.

Many children even outfitted their bikes so they could live the dream!

Breyer Animal Creations® began as the Breyer Molding Company, a Chicago, Illinois-based plastics manufacturing company. Its first model horse, the # 57 Western Horse, made its appearance in 1950. It was a special order for the F.W. Woolworth Company, made to adorn a mantelpiece clock. The company was then flooded with requests from people who saw it and wanted to know if they could purchase just the horse! By accepting that one order, the Breyer Molding Company had changed the focus of its business and company direction forever! *(cited from: https://www.breyerhorses.com/breyer_history)*

According to the American Horse Council, there are an estimated 2 million horse owners in the United States. There are 7.2 million horses, this includes both recreational and commercial horses. Out of the grand total, 3.91 million are used for recreational purposes, 2.72 million for showing, 1.75 million for other activities including farm work, rodeo, polo, police work, etc. and 840,000 are used for racing.

The equine sports included in the Olympics are Jumping, Dressage and Eventing. The World Equestrian Games (WEG), held every 4 years in between the Olympics, includes those disciplines as well as combined driving, endurance riding, para-dressage, reining and vaulting.

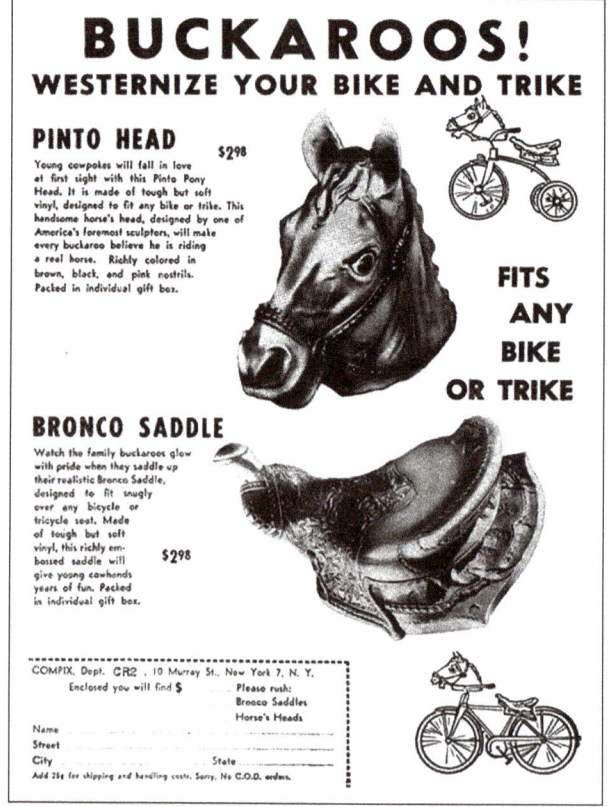

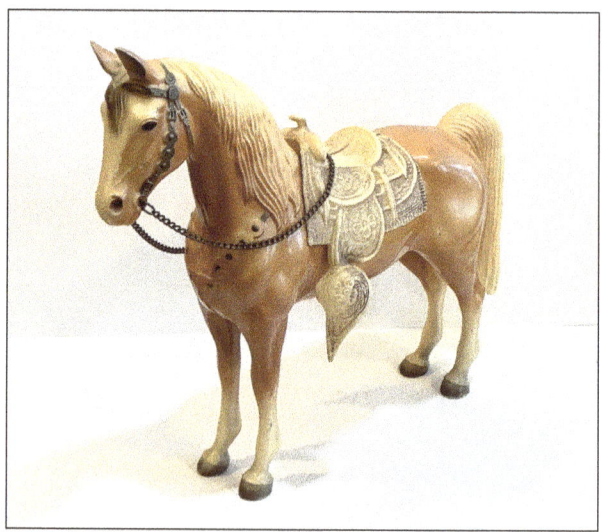

The first Breyer model horse, the # 57 Western Horse

The sport of Jumping

Dressage featuring Fuego XII at the 2010 WEG, sire of two of Gloria Austin's horses

Jumping is a sport where a horse and athlete jump a series of 1.6m fences in an arena setting while attempting to leave all the obstacles in place without knocking any of them to the ground. Riders who navigate the first-round track without accumulating any faults will move forward to the jump-off, which is a head-to-head competition to see who can complete the shortened course in the fastest time without adding faults.

Dressage is often compared to ballet, with a scoring system similar to ice skating. The harmonious connection between the human and equine athletes allows each pair to perform an intricate pattern of movements for which they receive scores from a seven-member judging panel. The Freestyle is performed to the music of the rider's choice, and spectators can expect to see incredibly complicated choreography performed in unison with the music.

The ultimate test of a rider's and horse's skills-set, Eventing, is often dubbed the "triathlon of equestrianism." It is a formidable combination of Dressage, Cross-country, and Jumping, done over 3 days, and with the same horse for each phase of the competition.

Combine Driving begins with the dressage phase, in which combinations must complete a test, judged on their accuracy and unison. Following dressage is Marathon, where you will get a taste of what wild chariot races must have felt like, as you watch turnouts navigate in and out of tight corners and turns. Driving concludes with the Cones phase, which tests the accuracy and speed of each horse and whip (driver) combination, as they navigate through cones with precisely placed tennis-ball like objects on top. If they knock a ball off a cone, they accrue additional penalty points.

Endurance is a long-distance competition against the clock. It tests the speed and stamina of both horse and rider and challenges each combination to ensure the effective use of pace and navigational skills of undulating terrains. Mandatory vet checks and rest periods are a key aspect of the competition and ensure horse and rider welfare throughout the 100-mile test.

Para-dressage is conducted under the same basic rules as conventional Dressage, but with riders divided into different competition grades based on functional abilities.

In Reining competitions, contestants are required to run one of several approved patterns, which are divided into 7 or 8 maneuver groups. Each pattern includes small slow circles, large fast circles, flying lead changes, rollbacks over the hocks, a series of 360-degree spins done in place, and the exciting sliding stops that are the hallmark of the reining horse.

For gymnastics enthusiasts, vaulting is a sister sport, but on the back of a horse. All vaulting routines—team, individual, and freestyle—are performed on the back of a cantering horse, traveling in a circle and attached to a lunge line. *(cited from: https://www.fei.org/stories/weg-2018-disciplines-explained)*

You don't need to be an Olympian to participate in any of these events. Horse shows featuring each of these disciplines are held all over the United States. In addition to the Olympics and World Equestrian Games disciplines, horse shows also feature many other disciplines.

There are many horse shows that are for specific breeds of horses like Morgans and Quarter horses. Classes offered include driving, English and Western riding, jumping, dressage, equitation in-hand (where the horse's conformation is judged), and much more. There are also equitation classes where the ability of the rider is adjudicated.

Western sports are often featured at rodeos and include barrel racing, pole bending, cutting, roping, and more.

Horse racing has been popular since colonial times. Most people are familiar with Thoroughbred racing such as the Kentucky Derby and Harness racing, but there are also races for Quarter Horses and Arabian horses.

Polo is a popular mounted team sport; many colleges have Polo teams. It is one of the world's oldest known team sports. Polo is played on a 300 by 160-yard grass field outdoors or a 300 by 150-foot dirt arena indoors. Players score by driving the ball between the opposing team's goalposts using a bamboo mallet while riding at speeds of up to 35 mph. The team with the highest score after 4 to 6 chukkers (periods) of play wins the game. If both teams are tied at the end of the final chukker, play will go into overtime. The game follows some established rules that keep the horses and riders safe. *(cited from: https://www.uspolo.org/sport/rules)*

Foxhunting is the chase of a fox by horsemen with a pack of hounds. In England, the home of the sport, foxhunting dates from at least the 15th century. To the earliest American colonists, fox hunting represented freedom. Back in England, most types of hunting were heavily regulated, with the best lands and species reserved for the king under penalty of death. George Washington was a fox hunter; so too, were Theodore Roosevelt, Jacqueline Kennedy, and Ronald Reagan. Andrew Jackson used to host post-hunt dinners at the White House. In the United States and Canada, the goal of hound-led hunts is typically not to kill the quarry; the emphasis is on the chase. In some areas, an increasing number of coyotes—which are bigger, faster, and stronger than foxes—are often hunted instead. *(cited from: https://www.washingtonpost.com/news/style/wp/2018/02/22/feature/will-a-new-generation-save-fox-hunting/?utm_term=.d73218e73dff)*

For many horse lovers, a trail ride with friends or camping with horses is the ultimate horse experience. Many children attend horse camps in the summer and learn the joys of spending time with a horse.

Horses are also used for therapy. Equine Therapy is a form of experiential therapy that involves interactions between patients and horses. Equine Therapy involves activities, such as grooming, feeding, haltering, and leading a horse that is supervised by a mental health professional, often with the support of a horse professional. Many of the benefits of equine therapy are likely due to the nature of the animals with which the patient and equine therapist are interacting. Horses are typically non-judgmental, have no preconceived expectations or motives, and are highly effective at mirroring attitudes and behaviors of the humans with whom they are working. *(cited from: https://www.crchealth.com/types-of-therapy/what-is-equine-therapy/)*

Horses 4 Heroes is an Equine Therapy program for Wounded Warriors. Different therapeutic riding programs for wounded soldiers can be found all over the USA. The program is being undertaken under the Professional Association of Therapeutic Horsemanship International (PATH International) after the successful pilot program in Fort Hood and Fort Meyer.

For some, just looking out the window and seeing a horse in the pasture or spending time grooming a horse is all that is needed to fulfill that childhood dream of owning a horse.

While horses no longer power the cities and farms of America, horses are still found in every state of America. Some are working horses on ranches, some are show horses earning ribbons and teaching their owners lessons of perseverance and patience, and some are pleasure horses doing just that–bringing pleasure to their owners by maybe doing nothing more than grazing in a pasture.

Many children grow up wishing to own a horse of their own someday - many of those wishes do come true!

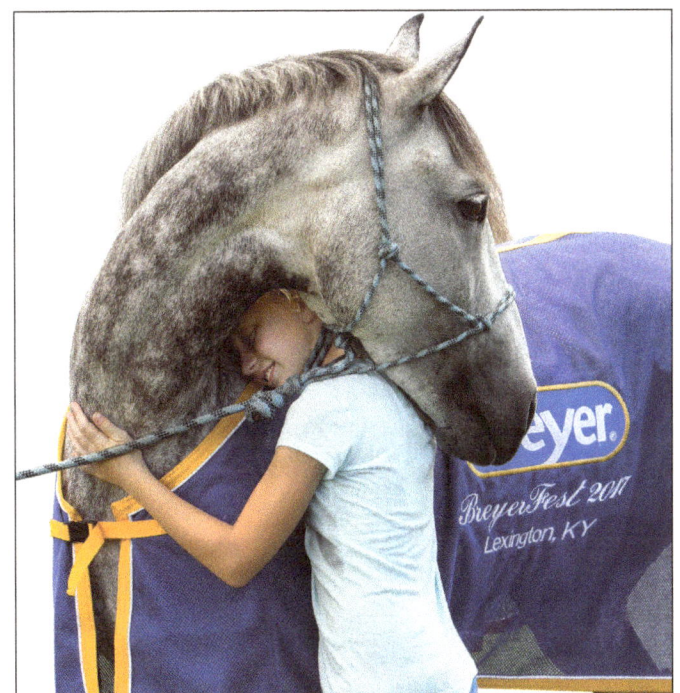

Sources

Books and Periodicals

Fisher, Vardis and Holmes, Opal Laurel (1968) Gold Rushes and Mining Camps of the Early American West, Caxton Press. p. 134

Levin, Jonathon V. (2017) Where Have All the Horse Gone? Jefferson, North Carolina. McFarland & Company, Inc.

Tarr, Joel. "Urban Pollution— Many Long Years Ago". American Heritage, 1971 Volume 22, Issue 6

INTERNET SOURCES

Miscellaneous

https://www.mountvernon.org/library/digitalhistory/digital-encyclopedia/article/nelson-horse/
https://www.americanheritage.com/content/fox-hunting-america http://www.providencejournal.com/opinion/commentary/20140207-robert-a.-geake-when-wolves-ranged-new-england.ece
http://www.history.org/Almanack/life/trades/traderural_horses.cfm
http://www.imh.org/exhibits/online/legacy-of-the-horse/colonial-horses/
http://www.imh.org/exhibits/online/legacy-of-the-horse/colonial-horses/
https://archive.org/stream/horseraisinginco00phil/horseraisinginco00phil_djvu.txt
https://www.americancowboy.com/ranch-life-archive/history-vaquero https://www.nationalgeographic.org/encyclopedia/ranching/
http://www.pbs.org/gunsgermssteel/variables/horses.htm
http://www.mexconnect.com/articles/682-the-aztecs-speak-an-aztec-account-of-the-conquest-of-mexico
http://www.boweryboyshistory.com/2011/05/why-go-to-kentucky-new-yorks.html
http://www.imh.org/exhibits/online/legacy-of-the-horse/colonial-horses/
http://www.imh.org/exhibits/online/legacy-of-the-horse/colonial-horses/
Descriptive Zoopraxograph, 1893, by Eadweard Muybridge) http://www.newenglandhistoricalsociety.com/narragansett-pacer-lost-horse-new-england-colonies/
http://www.imh.org
https://archive.org/stream/horseraisinginco00phil/horseraisinginco00phil_djvu.txt
https://www.fhwa.dot.gov/publications/publicroads/02janfeb/exhibition.cfm

Revolutionary Times

http://www.taxhistory.org/www/website.nsf/Web/THM1756?OpenDocument
http://philadelphiaencyclopedia.org/archive/horses/
https://www.paulreverehouse.org/the-real-story/

http://www.revolutionarywararchives.org/cavalry.html
http://www.equitrekking.com/articles/entry/sybil-ludington-and-her-horse-star-heroes-of-the-american-revolution/
https://www.encyclopediavirginia.org/Jack_Jouett_s_Ride_1781
https://www.awesomestories.com/asset/view/The-Horse-America-Throwing-His-Master-1779-Cartoon
https://www.thehistorycat-us.com/the-american-revolution
https://www.stratfordhall.org/meet-the-lee-family/henry-lee-iii/
https://www.u-s-history.com/pages/h1294.html

Advancing Frontier
http://www.lewis-clark.org/article/3342
https://truewestmagazine.com/the-mormon-handcart-migration/
https://www.farmcollector.com/farm-life/making-american-plow
http://www.historynet.com/mormon-handcart-horrors.htm
http://kentuckyancestors.org/the-untraveled-history-of-the-wilderness-road/
http://www.wondersandmarvels.com/2015/09/why-i-fell-in-love-with-sarah-royce-pioneer-woman-of-the-gold-rush.html
https://nationalponyexpress.org/historic-pony-express-trail/founders/
http://amhistory.si.edu/ourstory/activities/sodhouse/more.html
http://www.lrgaf.org/articles/ahta.htm
http://plainshumanities.unl.edu/encyclopedia/doc/egp.gen.040

Civil War
http://ushistoryscene.com/article/civilwaranimals/
http://www.thomaslegion.net/americancivilwar/totalcivilwarhorseskilled.html
http://www.civilwar.com/overview/315-weapons/148532-cavalry-62478.html
https://civilwar.mrdonn.org/supplytrains.html
https://www.civilwarhorses.net/links.php?326695
http://www.civil-war.net/cw_images/files/images/367.jpg
http://www.loc.gov/teachers/classroommaterials/presentationsandactivities/presentations/timeline/riseind/city

Growth of Cities / WWI / On the Move
https://ephemeralnewyork.wordpress.com/2012/01/24/the-horse-walks-hiding-in-greenwich-village/
https://ephemeralnewyork.wordpress.com/2012/12/08/lovely-fountains-for-city-horses-and-other-animals/
https://ephemeralnewyork.wordpress.com/2016/06/30/the-1904-horse-auction-house-in-the-east-village/

http://mentalfloss.com/article/83608/10-relics-horse-powered-city
https://www.sfmta.com/getting-around/muni/cable-cars/cable-car-history
http://www.foundsf.org/index.php?title=The_Heyday_of_Horsecars
https://courses.lumenlearning.com/ushistory2os2xmaster/chapter/urbanization-and-its-challenges/
https://theblobologist.wordpress.com/2013/05/12/horsepower/
https://www.horsetalk.co.nz/2014/02/17/how-equine-flu-brought-us-standstill/
https://blogs.loc.gov/picturethis/2015/10/work-horses-pulling-their-weight/
http://frozen61.tripod.com/id5.html
https://www.carriageassociationofamerica.com/coson-carriage-tour/gigs-carts/
https://www.carriageassociationofamerica.com/carriage-tour/stanhope-gig/
https://www.thehenryford.org/collections-and-research/digital-collections/artifact/27990
https://www.pantagraph.com/news/local/great-epizootic-of-brought-commerce-to-a-standstill/article_a7f6135b-6803-5018-aeb5-a8003f8b9759.html
https://fee.org/articles/the-great-horse-manure-crisis-of-1894/
https://www.rtbf.be/ww1/topics/detail_the-horse-an-essential-participant-of-the-great-war?id=8358614)

Horse Breeds in America

https://www.washingtonpost.com/lifestyle/kidspost/choctaw-horses-make-a-comeback-in-mississippi/2018/10/17/2b3d4a36-d16a-11e8-8c22-fa2ef74bd6d6_story.html
https://returntofreedom.org/what-we-do/sanctuary/our-horses/choctaw-herd/

America Today

http://www.horsecouncil.org/press-release/ahcf-announces-results-2017-economic-impact-study/
https://www.fei.org/stories/weg-2018-disciplines-explained
https://www.uspolo.org/sport/rules
https://www.washingtonpost.com/news/style/wp/2018/02/22/feature/will-a-new-generation-save-fox-hunting/?utm_term=.d73218e73dff
https://www.crchealth.com/types-of-therapy/what-is-equine-therapy/
https://www.breyerhorses.com/breyer_history